TEACHING WELL

How healthy, empowered teachers lead
to thriving, successful classrooms

Lisa Bush

Pembroke Publishers Limited

To Enrique

© 2019 Pembroke Publishers
538 Hood Road
Markham, Ontario, Canada L3R 3K9
www.pembrokepublishers.com

Distributed in the U.S. by Stenhouse Publishers
www.stenhouse.com

Funded by the Government of Canada
Financé par le gouvernement du Canada | Canada

Library and Archives Canada Cataloguing in Publication

Bush, Lisa (Lisa Christina), author
    Teaching well : how healthy, empowered teachers lead to thriving, successful classrooms / Lisa Bush.

Includes bibliographical references and index.
Issued in print and electronic formats.
ISBN 978-1-55138-337-8 (softcover).--ISBN 978-1-55138-937-0 (PDF)

    1. Teachers--Job stress--Prevention. 2. Burn out (Psychology)--Prevention.
3. Teachers--Workload. 4. Work-life balance. I. Title.

LB2840.2.B88 2019   371.1001'9   C2018-905898-6
                                                               C2018-905899-4

Editor: Alisa Yampolsky
Cover Design: John Zehethofer
Typesetting: Jay Tee Graphics Ltd.

Printed and bound in Canada
9 8 7 6 5 4 3 2 1

MIX
Paper from
responsible sources
FSC® C004071

Contents

Introduction

I used to think there were only two types of teachers.

The first type was the "good" teacher. With military precision, she issued a rapid stream of assignments, followed by non-negotiable deadlines. An impressive list of due dates was posted in red at the front of her class. She was the expert in the room, keeping a tight hold over her students. And once she released her iron grip to let students work, there was a frantic energy permeating her classroom as students typed as fast as their laptops would allow in an attempt to meet a looming deadline. As soon as one essay was completed, a business letter was due. And as soon as the business letter was completed, an exam hung on the horizon. Students would graduate from her class and enter the next grade proficient in the basic curriculum thanks to their teacher imposing constant deadlines. The students were competent. And the teacher was exhausted.

The second type of teacher was the, um, "questionable" teacher. Her students spent a suspiciously significant amount of time watching videos. Students were lulled into a trance from the blue lights of the movie reflecting from the SMART-Board. There was also a good deal of skits and group work in her classroom. Very little written work was done. This was the *fun class*. Students might not be able to identify a thesis or explain what a plot structure looked like at the end of the year. Or write. But they had a good time. And their teacher was happy. And sane.

So in my mind, I could be a "good," exhausted teacher or a "questionable" teacher with a life. That was it. Those were my only choices.

In my personal life, I always make it a rule to forge my own path and not worry about living up to social norms. I have no qualms about ripping out my front lawn and planting a vegetable garden. Or eloping. And then leaving the country permanently. But, for whatever reason, I did not feel confident finding my own path as a teacher. Possibly because it is my career and life calling. Possibly because it pays the bills so I can buy more zucchini plants for my front yard.

In retrospect, I realize that thinking there are only two types of teachers is just as absurd as thinking there are only two types of wildflowers or two types of gelato. Teachers possess an infinite number of unique attributes; we can forge our own rich, colorful identity. Educators do not only exist on opposing ends of a spectrum: "good" or "bad," "hardworking" or "lazy." It is possible to simultaneously challenge and engage our students while finding time to strengthen our own mental and physical health, to spend time with those we love, and to do what inspires us.

Five years ago, when I was pregnant with my first child and teaching full-time, I started re-evaluating the need for wellness in my life. As a middle school Language Arts teacher with a heavy marking load, this was not an easy task. I knew that my workload was draining me and that I needed to pursue a healthy quality of life. I needed to be an inspired, passionate educator (as opposed to an overworked, resentful educator).

I knew it was possible to be a healthy, fulfilled individual and a stellar teacher. I was fortunate enough to have been taught by an all-star lineup of middle school teachers. Mrs. Ellington, my Literature teacher, would light up the classroom the moment she walked into it. She wore brightly colored kaftans and red lipstick. She had four children, a busy social life, and was bursting with creative ideas. In her class, I constructed Mount Olympus out of papier-maché. After reading Homer's *Odyssey*, I learned how to sing the Greek alphabet to the tune of "A Spoonful of Sugar."

Mr. Davis, our Choir teacher, was impeccably dressed in his Windsor knot tie and starched dress shirts. His passion for music and joy for life were so contagious that even as a completely tone-deaf teenager I signed up for the choir. I just wanted to be with Mr. Davis. We all did.

Mrs. Delaski taught us Algebra in her running shoes and fleece vest looking like she had just come off of a hiking trail. Her cropped grey hair framed her face, which radiated health and balance. She would start every Math class giving us the latest updates on her son, who was a freshman at the Naval Academy. These stories usually contained an embedded message of strength, endurance, and perseverance.

Mr. Grunden, our Art teacher, brought in his extensive cassette tape collection, meticulously labelled in black handwriting, for us to listen to during class. (Yes, I am that old. To the young teachers reading this, cassette tapes are like your smartphone with two spools of plastic ribbon tightly wound…forget it. Just Google it.) He introduced us to R.E.M., Radiohead, and other fringe bands of the time. He often had his own easel set up in the corner, which he would work on before and after school.

I loved these teachers not only because they were masters in their field of teaching (which they absolutely were), but because they were happy, healthy, fulfilled individuals. And I wanted to bask in their happiness and their joy for life.

In the past 25 years or so, I might have come across this type of teacher a handful of times. But I did not know how to emulate them. I chalked them up to an anomaly, a rare genetic mutation resulting in a teaching superpower. And yet, I wanted to be this teacher. This teacher who could make her students work and create and learn without drowning in assessment and planning. I wanted to have a rich and fulfilling life outside the classroom. And in time, I would be this teacher or my own unique version of it.

Is This Book for You?

This book looks at creating a healthy and fulfilling lifestyle primarily by reducing the time spent working outside the classroom. It looks at how embracing a healthy lifestyle is not only beneficial to educators but to students, classrooms, and schools. The primary focus of the book is *why* we must make our wellness a priority and *how* to reduce the amount of time we spend working outside of school hours so that we are able to create that healthy life. Since I am a Humanities teacher there are many examples of how this would look in a Language Arts class, although many of the principles could be applied to other subject areas.

In essence, this book is for you if:

- You feel guilty about spending time with your family; going to the gym; or eating lunch; or taking a shower; or breathing—because you have lessons to plan and papers to mark.
- You have always wanted to play the trombone. Or write a novel. Or learn Portuguese. But you haven't because your "free time" consists of the 30 seconds between crawling into bed after a long day of work and falling asleep.
- You consider it completely normal to go into work when it is dark outside and leave work when it is dark outside. You remain positive by reassuring yourself that you could always play the role of an extra in a vampire thriller.
- "Winter break" and "spring break" are code for "time to catch up on my marking and plan for the next term."
- You have begun to accept that you spend more time with your red marking pen than you do with your best friend. And the idea of a "late night out" usually involves you and a stack of essays at a local coffee shop.
- You collect assignments from students that are so awful that halfway through marking you want to return them. Or burn them.
- You are an experienced teacher facing burnout. You want to ignite energy and passion into your own life as well as into your classroom.
- You are a new teacher and are completely flipping out at the number of assignments that need to be created, collected, and graded in a school year and consequently are thinking you should go into accounting instead.
- You have to leave photographs of yourself around the house labelled "MOM" or "DAD" so that your children can remember what you look like during the school year.

If you can relate to any (or all) of the above hypothetical situations, keep reading. You have come to the right place.

Ask Yourself:
- What do I hope to gain from this book?
- What is the driving force behind me reading this book?

Why Assessment?

I would like for education to be a field which the brightest minds in North America compete to join. I would like for brilliant writers, artists, historians, musicians, mathematicians, scientists, and engineers to think, *Ah, teaching: That is where I want to be.*

In order for that to happen, a slew of issues need to be addressed and corrected. These range from teacher compensation to workload to class size to the respect we as a society hold toward education in general. So with all of these issues looming about, why in the world am I writing about lightening our grading load? Why am I addressing such a minor issue when there are massive global issues that need to be addressed?

The answer is because, for teachers, grading is not a minor issue.

The answer is because when I was pregnant with my first child and teaching Grade 7, 8, and 9 Language Arts, Grade 8 Social Studies, and Grade 8 Religion, it was the marking that was pushing me to the edge. And when I speak with other teachers, it is often the marking that is the greatest and the most immediate source of stress.

Several years ago I started speaking at teachers' conventions around Alberta about how I significantly reduced the time I spent marking and planning as a Language Arts teacher. For the most part, these talks were packed with educators desperate to know how to work less. Not surprising, considering that the 2015 Alberta Teacher Workload Study concluded that teachers reported increasingly complex and challenging workloads, with less support staff than in the previous year. This study recruited 3,374 teachers to complete a time use diary where they would log their work activities at 30-minute intervals over the course of ten months. The study found that only 26% of teachers were satisfied with their "work–life balance." According to the Canadian Teachers' Federation, teachers in Canada work an average of 50–55 hours per week. This workload increases stress and leads to burnout.

When I was speaking at conventions, the feedback from teachers was inspiring. These educators confirmed that I was not alone with my time management conundrum nor was I alone with my discontent of the workload placed on teachers both inside and outside of the classroom. I began to accept that the problem of assessment was not unique to me nor was it a result of my own personal shortcomings. I began to accept that an overwhelming marking load is systemic in nature and primarily the result of increasing work demands, inadequate time for planning, and a lack of knowledge on how to assess efficiently. Which is not surprising given that "Spend less time marking essays!" or "Teachers can—and should—have lives too!" are not classes historically offered in university to pre-service teachers. Finally, feedback from educators confirmed that my solutions were plausible for a variety of classroom settings, ranging from elementary through university.

Assessment, unlike some of the larger global issues in education, is within our immediate power to correct. So instead of focusing solely on external constraints in education, I started to work on internal constraints or issues within my immediate control. What I told myself, and what I will tell you over and over and over again is this: Teachers working around the clock is neither good for our education system nor our students.

There are many insightful books on education currently available. They offer the best practices in transforming your classroom and your students' educational experience through proper assessment. While these books have their place in the educational system, what I have always wanted—what I have always *needed*—was a book on how to transform my life inside and *outside* of the classroom. During my teaching career, with the assistance of other teachers, graduate classes, professional development, trial and error, and yes, reading bits and pieces of books on assessment, I grew to understand how to fine-tune my assessment methods. I figured out how to assess project-based learning and group work. I could create a competent rubric for any given assignment. What I did not understand was how to stay on top of all these assessments while still having a life. I did not

Teachers working around the clock is neither good for our education system nor our students.

understand how to assess *and* go to the gym *and* spend time with my family *and* get eight hours of sleep per night *and* find time to write.

While many books offer you best practices in assessment, I am offering you the best practices in teaching and learning while putting your own wellness as a priority. This book is a creative approach to getting your life back while becoming an even more brilliant teacher than you are currently. You benefit. As do your students and your school. Ultimately, I hope this book will encourage you to not only look critically at the effectiveness of your teaching practices but also to re-evaluate your quality of life beyond your classroom.

What Is Wellness?

I don't eat kale. I have never taken a hot yoga class. And my favorite meal is steak served with fries smothered in ketchup. And yet I am writing a book on wellness (and for the record, I have crazy low blood pressure and low iron, so steak and fries could reasonably be considered "healthy" for me).

Fortunately, wellness looks different for everyone. While there are some common pillars to keeping ourselves well, such as sleep, diet, and stress reduction, what works for each of us will vary. For example, maintaining my wellness consists of daily small, solitary tasks that allow me to decompress: pulling weeds in my vegetable garden in the late evening light, writing, reading, or going for an early morning walk. Ideally, I combine these tasks with long-term creative projects: writing a collection of poetry, painting a series of Western Canadian landscapes, or writing a book.

If we are going to energize and inspire our students over the course of decades, we must make our mental and physical health a top priority.

Depending on where you are in your life, your need for wellness will fluctuate. Ironically, the more stressed and overworked we are, the more we need to focus on wellness, simply to maintain our general health and sanity. Those times where we feel like we have *no time at all* are the moments that we need to stop and put wellness front and centre in our lives. On the flip side, if you have a low-key job, a non-demanding personal life, and you are generally a relaxed, healthy, happy person, you might not need to put a whole lot of emphasis on your wellness. Unfortunately, I have yet to meet an individual working in education with loads of time and a low-stress job. Teaching is inherently one of the most non-stop, energy consuming careers out there. We ultimately are "on" for six to eight hours a day. Every day. Compound that with our personal and family lives, and things can get overwhelming quickly. Which is why wellness is key to career teachers. If we are going to energize and inspire our students over the course of decades, we must make our mental and physical health a top priority. Think of what wellness looks like to you. Be compassionate with yourself. Be gentle. Be kind. And realistic. In this book I tend to aim high when I speak of wellness—it is the teacher in me, I guess, always aiming for excellence. However, start at a place that feels right to you.

The Merriam-Webster dictionary defines wellness as "the quality or state of being in good health especially as an actively sought goal." I think the part that we need to key in is on the "actively sought goal." Wellness for teachers in the 21st century will have to be deliberate and planned. It will not happen accidentally or serendipitously. I have personally spent the last five years of my life in a focused and intentional pursuit of wellness. The good news is that it is possible to achieve. And once we make an effort toward wellness, the consequences are transformative.

When visualizing what your healthy life beyond the classroom looks like, allow yourself to dream. Teachers have a history of allowing their dreams to take on unique shapes. Teachers have also traditionally done an exceptional job of bringing those dreams to fruition. Clara Barton, the founder of the American Red Cross, taught in both Canada and the United States. Simone de Beauvoir, philosopher, feminist, political activist, and author of *The Second Sex*, taught high school for 14 years. Civil rights activist, artist, and children's book author Faith Ringgold taught in the New York public school system. Pop artist and social justice advocate Sister Mary Corita Kent taught primary school in British Columbia before moving to Los Angeles' Immaculate Heart school system. Singer Roberta Flack, best known for "Killing Me Softly," was a middle school music teacher. Sheryl Crow taught elementary school. Current Canadian Prime Minister Justin Trudeau taught Math and French in Vancouver. If teachers can find a way to reduce their all-encompassing workload and carve out some time to focus on their personal passions, the possibilities are endless.

Many teachers are also incredibly creative. They are visual artists or musicians or writers. If you pull a few books from your young adult (YA) class library, you will most likely be holding in your hands the works of former teachers. Philip Pullman, author of the fantasy YA trilogy, *His Dark Materials*, with epic protagonist Lyra Belacqua, was a middle school teacher in Oxford. Eoin Colfer, author of the Artemis Fowl series, was a primary teacher. William Golding, author of the brutally savage classic *Lord of the Flies*, possibly got his inspiration from his students. He was a high school teacher of English and Philosophy (keep that in mind when you think your own class is out of control). And my personal hero, J.K. Rowling, taught English as a Second Language in Portugal. It is nifty to consider her among our ranks of teachers even if she didn't have to deal with standardized testing or lunch supervision or angry parental e-mails.

Recently, a Canadian educational advocate said, "Your legacy as a teacher is always determined by what your students do." While at first glance it sounds nice, I have to disagree. I would like to change it to, "Your legacy as a teacher can be anything you want it to be." We are not empty vessels. We are not passive individuals who must invest all our time and energy into our work and wait for the successes of our students in order for our legacy to be realized. If your students do spectacular things as a result of your stellar teaching, all the better. But we should not be dependent on their actions to create our legacy.

While we give a part of ourselves (a *very large* part) to our students and our careers, we have a right to maintain another part. A part of our own. We have a right to live a rich and creative life beyond the classroom walls. After all, if teachers only gave to their students with no attempt to maintain their own identity, we would be missing the soulful, powerful sounds of Flack's "The First Time I Saw Your Face" or her incredible rendition of "Bridge over Troubled Water". The American Red Cross might never have come into existence. Our Prime Minister might be sitting in his classroom marking a pile of Math quizzes, hoping that one of his students would be his legacy instead of him running one of the most powerful countries in the free world.

Who Is Your Role Model?

There are many ways to approach teaching. Learn from others, be inspired by others. But do not try to emulate others. Create your own approach. No matter where you are in life now is a great time to forge your own way. One of my favorite painters is Grandma Moses. As one of ten children, she lived in rural New York and went on to raise five children of her own. She lived the majority of her life in the fairly traditional roles of "mother," "wife," and "farmer." Until she turned 70. That's when Moses decided to start painting. And get this: She managed to produce 2,000 paintings in her lifetime. As a self-taught artist, her work has been shown in over 250 exhibits in the United States and Europe, including at the Museum of Modern Art (MOMA). My point here is that it is never too late for you to change the way you work and live. And there is not one set way to approach your life. Fortunately, you do not have to do it alone.

I encourage you to find your role model or mentor to help you break the mold of what we might consider to be a "traditional teacher." After all, it is the 21st century. Time to throw tradition out the window. Or recycle it. Or compost it. Regardless, good riddance. Through social media, I have found a plethora of inspiring educators. These teachers write blogs, publish books, create podcasts, and are YouTubers. They are public speakers, social advocates, political activists, and experts in their field. Go online and start researching. Or if you are wonderfully original, forge your own path and create your own identity based on your personal vision.

Recognizing that there are a variety of educators with rich and diverse professional lives was significant in altering the way I viewed my role as an educator. Becoming active on social media with teachers around the world inspired me to find my own unique approach to balancing teaching with a creatively fulfilling lifestyle. These are just a small fraction of the dynamic, diverse, and inspiring educators that I admire. However, it is a good starting point. Since I am a Humanities teacher, many of them are as well. I hope you will find them inspiring as well.

INSPIRING EDUCATORS

Educator	Who They Are	Where to Find Them
Dave Burgess	Former high school History teacher. Founder of Dave Burgess Consulting. Author of *Teach Like a Pirate: Increase Student Engagement, Boost Your Creativity, and Transform Your Life as an Educator.*	www.daveburgess.com @ BurgessDave
Beckie Di Leo Ross	Art educator, artist, and designer. Recipient of the Prime Minister's 2018 Award for Teaching Excellence.	www.beckiedileo.com @ BeckieDiLeo
Adrienne Gear	Elementary school teacher. Author of multiple books, including *Reading Power: Teaching Students to Think While They Read* and *Powerful Understanding: Helping Students Explore, Question, and Transform Their Thinking about Themselves and the World Around Them.*	www.readingpowergear.com @ AdrienneGear
Jennifer Gonzalez	Former middle school Language Arts teacher. Blogger. Podcaster. Author of *Hacking Education: 10 Quick Fixes for Every School* and *The Teacher's Guide to Tech.*	www.cultofpedagogy.com @ CultOfPedagogy

Joy Kirr	Middle school Language Arts teacher. Author of *Shift This! How to Implement Gradual Changes for Massive Impact in Your Classroom.*	geniushour.blogspot.com @ JoyKirr
Jessica Lahey	Teacher. Host of #AmWriting podcast. Regular contributor to the *Atlantic* and the *New York Times*. Author of the *New York Times* bestseller, *The Gift of Failure: How the Best Parents Learn to Let Go So Their Children Can Succeed.*	www.jessicalahey.com @ JessLahey
Donalyn Miller	Former elementary school teacher. Co-founder of Nerdy Book Club. Author of *The Book Whisperer: Awakening the Inner Reader in Every Child.*	www.bookwhisperer.com www.nerdybookclub. wordpress.com @ DonalynBooks
Cornelius Minor	Former middle school teacher. Lead staff developer at the Teachers College Reading and Writing Project. Author of *We Got This. Equity, Access, and the Quest to Be Who Our Students Need Us to Be.*	@ MisterMinor
Pernille Ripp	Grade 7 Language Arts teacher. Blogger. Public Speaker. Founder of The Global Read Aloud. Author of *Passionate Learners: How to Engage and Empower Your Students* and *Passionate Readers: The Art of Reaching and Engaging Every Child.*	www.pernillesripp.com @ PernilleRipp
Starr Sackstein	High school teacher. Prolific writer. Author of *Peer Feedback in the Classroom: Empowering Students to Be the Experts; Hacking Assessment: 10 Ways to Go Gradeless in a Traditional Grades School;* and *The Power of Questioning: Opening Up the World of Student Inquiry.*	@ MsSackstein
John Spencer	Former middle school teacher. Professor. Writer. YouTuber. Creator. Author of *Empower: What Happens When Students Own Their Learning; Launch: Using Design Thinking to Boost Creativity and Bring Out the Maker in Every Student;* and *Making Learning Flow: Instruction and Assessment Strategies that Empower Students to Love Learning and Reach New Levels of Achievement.*	www.spencerauthor.com @ SpencerIdeas
Sarah Thomas	Technology coordinator. Creator of the EduMatch project, a grassroots organization connecting educators from around the world.	www.edumatch.org @ sarahdateechur
Jose Vilson	Teacher. Writer. Activist. Executive Director of EduColor. Author of *This is Not a Test: A New Narrative on Race, Class, and Education.*	www.thejosevilson.com www.educolor.org

Ask Yourself:
• Where do I hope to be both professionally and personally two years from now? Five years from now? Ten years from now? In 15 years? 20 years?

Make a list of goals for yourself and save them, taking them out every few months to refresh your focus.

I hope you will finish this book not only with a clear sense of how to begin a journey of physical and mental wellness but also a clear sense of what you hope to do with your newly acquired time. In my case, I decided to have a second child, write a book, spend as much time as possible with my husband and children, and work intensely on my own physical and mental health. I am confident that you will find something that equally fulfills and nurtures your soul.

1

The Need for Change

Listen to Reason

Experienced teacher Dawn Vaessen was fortunate. Years ago, during her first year of teaching, her principal kicked her out of school. You see, Vaessen was under the impression that the later she stayed at school, the better a teacher she was. And so she would often stay in her classroom well into the dark hours of the evening planning, marking, and preparing for the next day. Until an administrator put an end to it.

One afternoon at 4:00 pm her principal walked into the classroom and told Vaessen to go home. She explains, "My first year teaching my principal would say to me, 'No. You have to leave school. You have to have time for you. You need an escape and you can't take these kids home with you.'" The principal went on to explain that the next morning Vaessen needed to be back in the classroom and it needed to be *her* standing there. Not an empty vessel. Not a reflection of the students. But a person with her own interests, passions, and identity. That meant having an identity that is separate from school. Vaessen concludes, "She told me to leave school by 4:00 pm. And that is probably the best thing that anyone has done for me in my career."

Dawn Vaessen went on to become a master gardener, to write and publish a book on gardening, and to raise two beautiful daughters as a single parent. These are things that would have been nearly impossible to achieve if she had let school consume her.

I, too, was fortunate. My first year of teaching I received advice from an experienced teacher. She told me, "Lisa, there will always be work to do in your classroom. The work for teachers does not end. But at some point, you have to close the door and walk away from your classroom. Leave the work behind. You need to take care of yourself and not let the work consume you." That uber-wise teacher was also my mother. However, unlike Vaessen, I completely ignored the advice.

In 2001, during my first year teaching Art in an extremely challenging public middle school in the United States, I was working around the clock. I made no attempt at healthy decompression in my personal life. The consequences were dire. It took months to recover with family support, medication, and professional guidance. I almost left teaching forever. However, in time, I found my way back into the Art classroom with wellness tucked close to my heart. I kept it there until I moved to Canada to work as a Language Arts teacher in a congregated gifted program. In a new country, teaching a new subject in a highly competitive school, I felt the need to prove myself. And in my haste to prove myself as an "excellent" teacher, I let my wellness go again.

From Surviving to Thriving

As far as I can tell, teachers are working around the clock predominantly for two reasons:

1. We are devoted, passionate educators and so we throw ourselves into our work, giving our students and our job 150%—and feel guilty with anything less. We view working long hours as evidence of our devotion to teaching.
2. We have too many expectations put on us (planning, marking, progress reports, parent communication, documentation, preparation for standardized testing, after-school activities), and we don't know how to reduce our workload. We don't *want* to work long hours. We don't care one bit about ego, but we do not see any way around it.

And for many of us, it is a combination of the two.

Teacher Lorelie Haydt recently shared with me the idea that many excellent and devoted teachers put unrealistically high expectations on themselves. Haydt states, "I think teachers have several things that we mistakenly wear as a badge of honor. If I am not at school until all hours of the night working, I am not a good teacher. If I do not go home and worry about my students, I am not a good teacher...I think it is almost an ego thing."

I laughed when Haydt said this because as a Language Arts teacher I had been collecting every invisible badge of honor possible. I saw late nights marking, working weekends, and putting neatly inked grades in my gradebook as badges of honor. I saw a strictly run classroom with perfectly constructed assignments as badges of honor. I saw being the expert in the classroom, always prepared, always with an answer, as a badge of honor. I saw sacrificing my own physical and mental health and putting my own interests aside all as badges of honor that I could use as proof of my stellar devotion to teaching and to my students. And for a while, it worked.

On a good day, magic happened in my classroom. I felt a bit like a sorceress waving her magic wand in the air and casting my students under a golden spell to create. The hours I spent in the Language Arts classroom were frequently the happiest part of my day.

Although I would like to imagine myself as the unwavering Professor McGonagall keeping Hogwarts meticulously run with my sharp mind and keen wand abilities, it was not the case. I was much more like the well-meaning but overly enthusiastic British cartoon character Nanny Plum, who inadvertently flooded the Sea of Tranquility with jelly from her magical picnic basket. Like Nanny Plum, I had not figured out how to temper my magic spells. And so I would request, "Write an essay!" And POOF! A towering pile of essays would materialize on my desk. I would say, "Write a book reflection!" And POOF! Two boxes of book reflections would appear. "Create a project!" And POOF! Suddenly every available surface of my classroom was covered by beautifully created and unique projects. All waiting to be assessed. I was drowning under a pile of assignments, and I could not find my way out.

After a particularly challenging school year, in an attempt to justify or possibly quantify my exhaustion, I added up every grade in my gradebook. Seeing as how I detest this type of tedious numeric activity, I can only assume I was procrastinating the writing of my year-end report card comments. After I counted every assignment for every student that I had marked for the year, I was appalled. Guess how many there were? Three-thousand-four-hundred-and-thirty-three assessments for one year.

Yup, that's 3,433 assessments for *one year!*

A few of the assignments were multiple-choice or basic quizzes, but because I teach Language Arts, the majority of them were far more complex and time intensive to assess. And because many of the classes were part of a congregated gifted program where overachieving tendencies run rampant among students, it was not unusual for me to receive a 17-page *Divergent* fan fiction short story to grade or, on one notable occasion, a 76-page novella about a time travelling knight.

Yet I went along with it. At this point in the game, the long working hours were no longer an ego thing (I would have willingly turned in my badges for a better-balanced life). I was working the long hours because I did not know any other way to stay on top of my assessment and planning. Dumbing down my teaching or turning to worksheets or multiple-choice assessments was not an option. I did not want to compromise the creative, individualistic spirit of my classroom. So for years, I made it work. Every Friday I lugged my bag home full of assignments to be marked. I brought home boxes (plural) of journals, independent reading assignments, and stories to mark over winter or spring "break." I spent late nights and early mornings filled with one of two emotions. 1. Guilt for not marking whatever assignment was currently piled on my desk. Or 2. Frustration when marking my students' work, which was all too often hastily composed and rushed in order to meet my imposed deadline.

In my quest to simply survive I had given up the things in my life that inspired me, that instilled a sense of passion in me. In my previous life, before studying the works of Jacqueline Woodson or S.E. Hinton with my students, I was studying the works of Alice Neel and Frieda Kahlo in my studio. I was an actively practicing visual artist and Art teacher. When I was an Art teacher I had a home studio. I usually had one or more paintings in progress waiting for me when I returned home for work. Occasionally I would receive a commission or have a small showing of my work.

Ask Yourself:
- What have I "packed up" from my previous life due to my marking or workload?
- What hobbies or activities would I like to "unpack" and incorporate back into my life?

When I became a Language Arts teacher, the wooden easel gathered dust until I folded it up and placed it, along with my well-worn shoebox full of tubes of paint, in a corner of the basement. I then converted my painting studio into a home office—it seemed a more practical use of space. I also packed up my social life, my time with my husband, and a large chunk of my sanity. I had no time for them either. I was not living a healthy life on any level. In regard to my personal well-being, September through June was a time of survival. The summer was a physical, emotional, and mental recovery period. This dysfunctional relationship between myself, my students' assignments, and my workload continued until it could continue no more: my husband and I decided to start a family. With a child on the way, I needed a change. As a teacher, and soon-to-be mom, I wanted to do better than survive. I wanted to flourish. I wanted to thrive.

Embrace Change

When I became pregnant with my first child, my energy levels plummeted. I felt that at any moment during the day I could put my face down on my hard, cluttered desk and fall into a drool-worthy sleep under the glare of the classroom's fluorescent lights. Just making it through the school day was an Olympic-level task. Trying to get myself out of bed in the morning was a Herculean task that I felt deserved a medal (for the record, I am still waiting for that medal). Staying up late into the night, trying to keep on top of marking was an impossibility. Heck, getting my shoes on without assistance was an impossibility.

During this time, I became so frustrated with my marking load, I not only wanted to leave teaching, I wanted to leave education altogether. I was too worn out to have any semblance of an ego. I was practically waving my invisible sash with years of badges sewn onto it shouting, *Take this away from me. I don't want it any longer. I want my health. I want to laugh. I want my life back!* I was torn. I could leave a career that I enjoyed or I could change everything I knew about teaching to make it something that could allow me to have a healthy lifestyle and time with my family. I knew both options were difficult, and I am glad to say that I chose the latter: I would change my approach to teaching.

Before we can take the first step toward change we have to admit a few things:

1. I need to change.
2. The way I look at learning needs to change.
3. The way I run my class needs to change.
4. In order to be the most loving, kind, compassionate, and overall brilliant teacher possible, I need a healthy life outside of school.

> If we are going to be in the teaching profession for years—or decades—wellness is not a luxury. It is a basic necessity.

And we have to believe it! We have to truly want—and be willing to advocate for—a change in lifestyle. If we are going to be in the teaching profession for years—or decades—wellness is not a luxury. It is a basic necessity.

Psychologist Simone McCreary argues that we need to get rid of the idea that wellness or taking the time to take care of ourselves is indulgent. In a recent conversation, McCreary advocated for the need for wellness stating, "There is plenty of evidence that we do better in our career when we make self-care a priority, even if it feels indulgent at the time. Regular physical activity activates our neuroplasticity, which increases our creativity and focus. Exercise rejuvenates our willpower."

Goodness knows in the teaching profession, with a class full of vulnerable ears listening to your every remark and testing your reactions, willpower is high up on the list of teachers' priorities. So not only are we more likely to have professional and compassionate commentary with our students when we practice self-care, but by taking time to take care of ourselves, chances are, we will actually get *more* done. McCreary explains that if we have a four-hour morning and we take one hour off to exercise, we might actually get *more* done than working four hours straight. If we are sitting for four hours at our desk, trying our best to be focused, creative, and productive, we might only get two hours' worth of work done because we are spinning our wheels, tired, anxious, or distracted.

Christine Brownell is a mental health nurse and nursing professor who is also a believer in the importance of wellness. She has spent her life studying mental health and traditional healing practices. She, like McCreary, acknowledges that we need to change our mindset in terms of wellness. She states, "In western society, we are quite challenged in thinking about our own health or our own needs on a very basic level. We think more about what we want to *attain*. What we want to *be*. What we want to gather around us, whether that be worldly possessions, or a special job title, or a dynamic career. But the challenge is that if you are not well in your mind, body, and spirit, how can you live a life in its fullest capacity?"

Brownell admits that when we are stressed and have many things pulling for our attention, it goes against our natural inclination to say, *Okay, I need to stop and go for a walk*, or *I need to lay down on my couch and read an engrossing novel for 20 minutes.* When we stop to take care of ourselves, our entire body seems to revolt yelling, *I haven't got time for this!* But we need to make time. Not only for ourselves, but for the sake of our students, our families, and our partners. According to Brownell:

> A lot of non-western philosophies believe that self-care is essential not only to your career but also in your relationships with others. It is taught that you need to do work on yourself in order to be at your fullest potential. But for some reason, we have in our current culture this belief that any time we do work on ourselves, we are being selfish. Or we are not using our time wisely. If we were to step out of ourselves and look at the greater perspective, then you would see that you actually will be more productive by going to that hour-long yoga class or taking that half-hour bath. You actually will be more patient as a parent. You actually will be more creative as a teacher. And it's funny because we think that self-care takes away from all of the other demands. And we forget that if we are running on empty our body and our mind and spirit continue to run on fumes. We are going to actually see that our body, mind, and spirit will start to feel as if they are crumbling. And that is when we do see things like perhaps, illness. Or perhaps someone's inability to find compassion anymore. Or creative lows. All of these sorts of things occur when we think we can run on fumes.

Wellness is key for us to be productive teachers, parents, and partners. It is also essential to our basic physical health. Registered Nurse and private medical practitioner Lisa Hildebrand agrees. When we give our energy to our students, our co-workers, and our school, when we stay up late night after night to mark papers, when we borrow tomorrow's energy units every single day, we eventually run out of gas and are operating completely on fumes. This is when Hildebrand starts to see severe health ramifications in her clients: fatigue, sleep troubles, digestive issues, anxiety, hormonal imbalance, and hypothyroidism.

As educators, we have things in our life that are *important* (e.g., going to the gym, eating healthy meals, and managing stress) and things in our life that are *urgent* (e.g., report card comments that are due at 9:00 am tomorrow or tests that need to be photocopied for next period's class). While our health, relationships, and mental and physical well-being might not be urgent, if we put them off or ignore them altogether, they will manifest themselves in urgent forms. If we ignore our need to sleep seven to eight hours a night (important), we might get the flu and be out for school for a week (urgent). If we ignore our need to release daily tension through self-care activities (important), we might be so emotionally worn thin that we have to take a stress leave (urgent). We must put our wellness as a daily priority. Otherwise, there will be urgent ramifications. I appreciate author David Irvine's direct approach and think it is especially applicable to teachers. He says, "Self-care is more than a luxury. Self-care is a responsibility. If we don't take care of ourselves, we eventually won't be able to carry the responsibility of caring for others."

Ready to dive into wellness, but unsure of where to start? See Four Pillars of Wellness. According to Hildebrand, these four pillars are the most basic, necessary aspects of wellness.

FOUR PILLARS OF WELLNESS

Wellness Pillar	Putting It into Action
1. Prepare for a good night's sleep.	Honor your body by going to sleep. Shut off your screens an hour before bed. Turn off Netflix. Put away the lesson plans. Do something you enjoy during the last hour of the evening. Read a great book. Have some tea. Take a bath. Stretch. Don't have guilt about going to bed. Teachers often talk to students about the importance of sleep. It is important to heed our own advice.
2. Manage stress.	Manage your daily stress by filling your bucket. Remember what you used to love to do and start doing it again. Whatever puts a smile on your face. Maybe you love to walk outside. Or read. Or garden. It can be anything. Something you love to do *just for the sake of doing it*. Not something that *has* to be done or that *needs* to be done. Do something just because you love to do it. Do this *daily*. If you are carrying around baggage or stress that you cannot seem to manage, don't suppress it or ignore it—consider getting professional help.
3. Put nutrients into your body.	Meet your nutrient demands. Teachers often get to the end of the day and are exhausted because they have not eaten enough calories throughout the day. Implement strategies in your life to make this possible. Buy pre-cut and prepared vegetables or make salads on Sunday for the first few days of the week. Have a nutrient-dense smoothie and sip on it in between classes. Pack things that you can pick up quickly and eat. Eat foods that you can put into your body that will actually give you energy and sustain you as opposed to those that will give you a quick jolt of energy that will drop at 3:00 pm when all of your after-school responsibilities kick in. Ensure that you are feeding yourself nutrient-dense foods at regular intervals throughout the day.
4. Stay hydrated.	Water is essential to health. Put down the coffee and sip water throughout the day. Drink enough water so that your urine is clear and pale yellow in color. For every one cup of coffee or caffeinated tea that you drink, your body needs four additional cups of water to balance the loss.

Changes in Your School Environment

If we want to be the best possible versions of ourselves, we must put our wellness as teachers as a top priority. We must view wellness as essential to our productivity and longevity in the teaching field. And we should strive to work in an environment that honors the health and wellness of its teachers. For many of us, that might mean that we need to be the ones to create a culture of wellness in our school. Wellness and empowerment go hand-in-hand. Once you start focusing on taking care of yourself, you feel better, you have more energy, and you are happier and more confident in yourself—you, in essence, become empowered. And that is a great thing. You will need a bit of empowerment to change a school culture.

Widen the Lens

Last summer my family and I travelled through Spain for two months. My husband Enrique was doing preliminary research for a book on the art and architecture of Spain. In preparation for the trip, he took a few photography courses and on the advice of his teachers purchased a wide-angle lens. It was expensive, but his teacher insisted it was necessary for photographing architecture. Initially apprehensive of its value, I was soon won over by the beautiful panoramic pictures that Enrique took using the new lens. Suddenly the snapshots that we took in Spain with our phones or with a regular lens seemed claustrophobic and uncomfortable. Those pictures looked tight and incomplete.

It is my experience that school districts and school administrators are inclined to zoom in on the wellness of their students while negating to see the importance of the wellness of their staff. The saying, "It's in the best interest of students" is something that I hear consistently—usually used in context to justify asking a teacher to take on more work. And while I agree that we should *always* look at what is in the best interest of students, we should do it with a lens that acknowledges a school is only as strong as its teachers and staff. Moreover, wellness is reciprocal in that what a school does to promote the happiness and health of its staff will directly benefit its students. After all, joy, passion, and positive outlooks are all contagious, or in the terms of Brownell, "Fantastic, infectious things."

We need to encourage our school districts and administrators to widen their lens. This does not have to be done in large, intimidating ways; rather it can be done through small, but powerful steps.

Start the Conversation

One thing that I did do well, once I decided to change, was talk to every person around me who would stop and listen about my need for change with my unmanageable workload. I unapologetically had two-hour long meetings with district employees, Language Arts consultants, my Language Arts colleagues, and administrators, all asking the question, "How can I be an excellent teacher *and* have a healthy life?"

If you decide to change the way you teach in order to run a more effective classroom and have a life, talk to others. Explain the importance of wellness. Take small steps in your school to bring focus and attention on having well-rounded teachers. Make the changes in your class public to others. Proudly explain to your co-workers and administrators that you are running a more effective classroom so that you can leave school and go home and have a well-balanced life. And then do it. Go home to exercise. Or spend time with your family. Or go to a painting class. Or a creative writing class. Now that is one badge of honor I would like to wear. The following table includes ideas for promoting teacher wellness that have been implemented in schools that I have worked in over the years.

Ask Yourself:
- Who in my life encourages me to take care of myself?
- How good am I (on a scale of 1–10) at encouraging myself to have a healthy life outside of work?
- How supportive are my administrators or co-workers at looking holistically at teacher well-being?
- Currently, is there any discussion or dialogue in my school about teacher well-being?

Activity	Putting It into Practice	Real-Life Examples
Start a walking group.	Get a group of teachers together and walk on a regular basis.	In our school, the walking groups tend to be informal. But since our school property backs onto a gorgeous natural park, there is always a small group of walkers. A group of two teachers and myself walk during our lunch while another teacher and I schedule walking dates after school.
Organize a group fitness class.	Hire a fitness instructor to come to your school to teach classes.	One year, a group of teachers hired a Pilates instructor to come to our school twice a week to teach lessons in our gym immediately after school. It was positive peer pressure at its best. Rarely did I miss a class—we held each other accountable.
Initiate a 30-day exercise challenge.	Invite all staff members to participate in a daily exercise challenge for 30 days.	This challenge can be 30 days or whatever length you want it to be. One year, an administrator started this and hung a chart up on the wall. If you wanted to sign up, you just added your name and put a shiny star sticker (we are teachers—what did you expect?) next to every day you exercised. This hung in our staffroom and created a visual reminder of the importance of exercise. It also promoted conversation during lunch about how much we were (or were not) exercising. Finally, it gave us an excuse as a staff to leave work daily at a reasonable time to make it to the gym—we were participating in an administration-initiated wellness activity.
Begin a professional development day with an hour of physical activity.	Take the first hour to exercise on a day scheduled entirely for meetings.	One professional development day, our principal set the first hour aside for exercise. It made such an impact on me, I will remember it for years to come. We had the option of going for a walk, playing a basketball game in the gym, or taking a teacher-led yoga class. When we started our meetings that morning I felt alert and relaxed because I had time first thing in the morning for myself. Additionally, like McCreary pointed out, we were likely more productive taking one hour out of our long day of meetings to exercise because our minds were focused and our ideas were flowing.
Join forces with co-workers to make healthy lunches.	Partner up with a co-worker or organize a group to help supply healthy lunches.	At one school in our district, five teachers got together and formed a "lunch club." Each teacher was responsible for bringing in a healthy nutrient-dense lunch for themselves and their four co-workers one day a week. The other four days, their co-workers would bring lunches for them. This can cut back significantly on the amount of time you have to spend making your lunch and forces you to eat healthy meals. If you do not have four other staff members at your school who are interested, you can just partner up. Two teachers last year got together and made their own "lunch club." Every Monday they brought in pre-cut vegetables, salads, salad dressings, fruit, and protein. They would stash it in our staff refrigerator and share it with each other throughout the week.
Bring in an expert to speak to staff about wellness.	During a professional development day or a staff meeting, bring in a psychologist or mental health expert to speak to staff about wellness.	This past year, our school had a professor come in and talk to us about how our brain responds to stress, exercise, sleep, and exposure to electronic devices. Not only was the talk fascinating but it shifted our focus away from curriculum and testing to the importance of wellness in both our students' lives and in our own life.

Have authentic discussions about assessment.	Use professional development days to come up with strategies to reduce time spent on marking.	One year our school's professional development focus was on assessment. It was teacher-led and practical—so teachers were sharing a lot of their own success and frustrations with each other. During this time, it was made clear to us by our administration that it was not the *quantity* of grades that we had so much as the *effectiveness* of our assessment methods. It gave us permission to experiment with assessment—and to not mark everything.
Talk to your administration about "working smarter not, harder."	At the beginning of the year, sit down with your administration to discuss wellness.	At the beginning of the year, ask your administration if you can have shared planning time with your team to share resources and reduce the amount of time you spend creating lessons. Or discuss the possibility of team teaching with others in your grade. Make it known right from the beginning that your focus is working smarter, not harder. The first conversation I had with my new principal was on assessment. I made sure he was on board with having few assessments in the gradebook as long as they were quality assessments covering multiple outcomes. He was my principal for five years and I knew from our first week's conversation that he was on board with my working smarter, not harder.
Ask for help.	Ask your subject consultants to come in and talk with you and your team about strategies for managing your workload.	Through numerous conversations with our district's consultants, I have figured out solutions to my most complex Language Arts questions: How can I reduce my marking? How do I reduce my overall workload? I have come to see our consultants as invaluable resources for wellness (I consider them the therapists for the Language Arts classroom!) My only regret is that I did not reach out to them earlier in my career. Please feel free to ask for help at any point in your career.

In-School Fitness Classes for Teachers

At my school, teachers and parents offer exercise classes. For example, on Monday, it's a free-circuit training class that another teacher, the Director of Athletics, does for us. On Tuesday, there is a high-intensity class just for teachers. There are also yoga classes, a Pilates class during the week, and also a boot camp. So, for exercise, there are lots of choices for activities without leaving the school.
–Jill, Grade 2 Teacher

Be the Role Model in Your School

One way to change your school's culture is to be the teacher who looks after herself. Find others in your life who take care of themselves. Surround yourself with positive, healthy influences. When you see a co-worker who looks after herself and fills her bucket, you will realize that you can do that too. And the more people that we have in our lives like that, the more likely we will be to emulate them.

If we show our students, our administration, and our family that *I am important, I deserve self-care*, and that *I am an equal member of this community in terms of what my physical, mental, and emotional body requires*, then our students, administration, and family will see that and it will become their expectation. And when that becomes their expectation things will change in regard to expectations placed on teachers. So, one way to change the school culture is to lead by example. And show others that it is okay. That we are not being selfish. It is self-preservation.

The advantages of living a life centred around the idea of wellness will directly benefit your school and your students.

The advantages of living a life centred around the idea of wellness will directly benefit your school and your students. Which makes sense when you think about it. A teacher and her class are interconnected—in order to change what is happening inside a classroom, it is beneficial to focus holistically on the teacher's life.

A holistic approach to creating change is not a new concept. When well-known financial advisor Gail Vaz-Oxlade counsels couples who are in debt, she looks beyond their bank statements. She looks in their closets, in their pantries, and in their basement. She examines their personal attitude toward money and toward each other before she gives them any sort of advice. She looks holistically at their life.

Likewise, when *Lean In* author and feminist Sheryl Sandberg examines why two generations after the feminist movement so few women are leading companies or countries, she looks holistically at the issue. Not only does she look at gender bias in the boardroom, but also in our home life, starting from how we interact with infants all the way through to unspoken expectations in marriage.

While terms like *empowered*, *engaged*, and *passionate* are used consistently to describe our students, they are not as frequently used in regard to educators. (A Google search for "empowered students" brought up 41 million results; "empowered teachers" brought up 18 million). A holistic approach should be used with education as well. Asking a teacher to create passionate, empowered learners, and to engage her students while negating to address the issues of whether she is a passionate, empowered, or engaged individual is not an effective approach to education.

Still not convinced that taking care of yourself will make you a better teacher? Then read on! The following chapters will widen our lens even further to look at all aspects of your professional and personal life as they relate to your wellness. Because I think a holistic approach to personal wellness is mandatory, I go to some places you might not expect. (I bet you did not expect an educational book to discuss who does the laundry and the grocery shopping in your household!)

In **Chapter 2: Why Wellness?** we look at how putting our wellness as a priority creates a healthier classroom environment and promotes creativity within our students. We look at the reciprocal relationship between a teacher's health and the health of her class.

In **Chapter 3: The Benefits of Collaboration**, we explore how to work smarter, not harder with the help of co-workers. Interested in having fewer core classes to plan for? Interested in having help with meeting the needs of your diverse student population? This chapter offers solutions.

Many of our concepts about learning are outdated or altogether incorrect. **Chapter 4: Thriving Classrooms** explores step-by-step how to get rid of ineffective lessons. We look at how to rebuild your long-range plans, both to maximize student learning and minimize time spent marking outside the classroom. We look at why we need to pass onto students the responsibility of learning and let go of some control on the class.

Chapter 5: Preps and After-School Time explores how to make the most of the time we spend preparing for classes so that we can get out of school and live a full and healthy life.

And finally, in **Chapter 6: Shifting Expectations**, we look at how to change the way we view teachers as a society. We examine how to change the expectations we put on ourselves as teachers, parents, friends, and spouses in order to live the fullest life possible.

My hope is that at the end of the book, you will have a very clear idea of how to embrace wellness in your life, your teaching, and with your students. So, let's dive in!

2

Why Wellness?

We Need to Practice What We Teach

While it was easy for me to recognize the benefits of sleeping well, eating nutrient-dense food, and staying hydrated, the idea of self-care or filling my bucket was a bit more difficult for me to buy into. For years I labelled self-care as "something nice to do if you have the time, but not mandatory." For years I ignored the advice of others and considered it a luxury. And when I finally went to a professional to manage my own stress and the stress in our family due to health issues, her response that I needed to go out with a close friend for have dinner or hire a babysitter and spend time with my husband completely baffled me. It again went back to self-care.

So if you are wondering, *How could taking the time to lose myself in a novel every night benefit my teaching? How would signing up for a yoga class or training for a half marathon make me stronger in the classroom? How would carving out the time to write poetry or work in my vegetable garden make me a more valuable co-worker?* I completely get you. I was there too.

Once I started looking for the answers, the results were more varied and more significant than you might expect. The first result being that simply, *We need to practice what we teach.* For example, if we ask our students to create, shouldn't we be creators ourselves? If we ask our students to take risks in the classroom, shouldn't we be willing to take risks in our lives outside the classroom?

Not long after I began to put my wellness as a priority, I came across the book, *Big Magic: Creative Living Beyond Fear* by *Eat Pray Love* author Elizabeth Gilbert. Gilbert explains that it does not matter what our age or what the outcome is, we as people have it intrinsically embedded in us to create. She points out that we have been making art for approximately 40,000 years while agriculture has only been around for 10,000 years. Therefore, humans found it more important to slap paint on cave walls than to have access to a consistent food supply. Yet even though it is engrained genetically in our DNA, that does not make the creation process any less terrifying. Gilbert writes, "Trust me, your fear will always show up—especially when you're trying to be inventive or innovative. Your fear will always be triggered by your creativity because creativity asks you to enter into realms of uncertain outcome, and fear *hates* uncertain outcome."

Taking Risks

We ask our students to create a structure made out of toothpicks and hot glue. *Uncertain outcome.* We ask our students to recite a poem in front of the class. *Uncertain outcome.* We ask our students to compete in a debate. *Uncertain outcome.*

As a teacher, the uncertain outcome for my students is an adrenaline rush. The lack of knowing how my students will resolve the challenge that I have given them is one of the things that keeps me showing up day after day excited to be there. However, the uncertain outcome can be paralyzing for students.

Several years ago, my Grade 7 students were reading their original poems in front of the class. The class was selecting five students to represent them in our annual poetry slam. I was sitting in the back of the room observing. Tony, a quiet, polite student got up to present. He stood in front of the class and looked out at his audience. His expression was remarkably similar to a deer in headlights. He stood deadly still for a long moment, then unexpectedly started to jump up and down. He did a few jumping jacks, jogged in place, and then shook his arms and legs while doing rapid Lamaze-type breathing. Finally, with a relieved smile on his face, he said, "Okay, much better. I'm ready."

I, along with the entire class, began laughing hysterically at his unexpected poetry warm-up routine. But after reflecting for a moment I was surprised. I found myself thinking, *Really, Tony, what is there to be so nervous about? You are in front of a supportive group. You are just reading a couple of poems. What's the big deal?*

That very week I was scheduled to read my own poetry at a local bookstore. The audience consisted of my husband, a few close friends, and some other local poets and their guests. I, essentially, was in the exact same situation as Tony— reading a few poems in front of a small supportive group. What was the big deal?

And yet...

When it was my turn to read, I went to the front of the room and looked out at the audience. My stomach dropped. My mouth turned dry. My heart started pounding. I could feel the sweat beading from my pores. I felt hot and cold simultaneously. I wanted to run. Or disappear into a hole in the ground. Seeing as how neither was a viable option, I did what seemed like the most logical thing. I started to jump up and down. I did a few jumping jacks. I jogged in place and then I shook my arms and legs while doing rapid Lamaze-type breathing. Finally, I said, "Okay, much better. I'm ready."

It was not until I was involved in a creative endeavor myself that I *got* where Tony was coming from. I understood the pressure and anxiety that shows up during the creation process when the outcome is unknown. This is the same creation process that I ask my students to do on a daily basis. To create can be exhilarating. It can be a rush. But it can also be a terrifying experience. If we ask our students to create, shouldn't we be living a creative life outside of the classroom?

Ask Yourself:
- What is the last thing I asked my students to create?
- When is the last time I created something? What did I create? How did the process make me feel?
- Did the creative process affect the way I taught? If so, how?

Fulfilling Your Dreams

How many times have you encouraged your students to "dream the impossible"? An excellent teacher will instill in students the confidence to articulate their dreams and the knowledge of how to work toward achieving them. She will be able to look her students in the eye and say, "Yes, you can." But here is the thing—that teacher must also be living a fulfilled life. She must be achieving a dream of her own.

Poet Langston Hughes was a literary force and prolific writer in the 20th century. My personal favorite work is his poem, *Harlem*. In it, he warns the reader of what happens when a dream is not fulfilled. Hughes cites several possibilities, all with dire outcomes: the dream dries up, it festers, it sags…or it explodes. On a societal level, its allusions to racial tensions in the city of Harlem, as well as in the country and the world, as the dream of racial equality is indefinitely "deferred." However, this can also resonate on a personal level. When we articulate our dream and actively work toward achieving it, we will be optimistic; we become the best possible versions of ourselves. However, when we set aside our dream day after day because school consumes all aspects of our life…well, it does not end well.

The happiest I have ever been in my life is when I have been simultaneously teaching and creating art. Or simultaneously teaching and writing. I walk into the classroom absolutely excited and thrilled to be there after a long night spent writing. I think to myself, *I spent last night writing—now it's my students' turn to give it a try.*

However, when I go months or years without tapping into my own creative dream, in the words of Langston Hughes, I sag. Like a heavy load. I go into workday after day after day not particularly excited to be there. Or I explode. My resentment spews out to my students. I think to myself, "They don't appreciate me" or "They don't appreciate my time."

> ### My Love of Gardening
>
> I am a much better teacher when I am writing and gardening because that is my escape. And I bring that passion to my work. When I write, I write for me. I garden for me and that is my escape. I totally nerd out. I love it. A few years ago I was yelling at my kids for something and my oldest daughter said, "Go out and garden. Because you are a nicer person when you garden."
> –Dawn, Grade 7, 8, and 9 Teacher

Artist, writer, and creativity guru Susan Ariel Rainbow Kennedy (known by her pen name SARK) notes that when people are living their dreams, there is an uplifting and refreshing quality about them. You feel a positive joy in their presence. They create more energy. They "sparkle." But SARK goes on to note that those who are not tapped into their creative dreams will lag. They will barely have the energy to function day to day and not much to give to others. She writes, "The world will benefit immensely from more people living their dreams. These people will be able to offer solutions and creative thought to long-standing problems and challenges." Actively living out your creative dreams fuels your creativity and problem-solving ability. And if there are two qualities that every teacher should have an ample supply of it is creativity and problem-solving.

It is difficult at best—and often impossible—for us to inspire our students to follow their dreams if our own dreams have been deferred.

By running a more efficient classroom and creating more time for yourself, you can now tap into your dreams. Start that book. Start focusing on your ideal teaching position. It is difficult at best—and often impossible—for us to inspire our students to follow their dreams if our own dreams have been deferred. Langston Hughes knew what he was talking about.

Finding Your Passion

If I could go back in a time machine to my first year of teaching and bring only one book with me to guide my experience, it would be *Teach Like a Pirate* by Dave Burgess. When I picked up this book a few years ago, I was hooked. In the book, Burgess, like so many educational consultants, talks about having passion in your teaching. Yet unlike many consultants, instead of simply saying, "Be passionate!" and then moving on leaving us all to wonder, *Where in the world do I get this passion from?* Burgess explains it.

Burgess gives several sources that you can draw on as a source of passion: your passion for education, your passion for the content you teach, and finally your personal passion. Burgess, for example, loves magic tricks and origami. Consequently, he finds a way to incorporate them into his high school History class whenever possible. Burgess writes:

> Almost every personal passion can be incorporated into the classroom...If you are passionate about playing the guitar, bring it in and play. I know teachers who have an incredible interest in cutting-edge technology. They find ways to incorporate their tech skills into their lessons. Bringing your personal passion to the classroom empowers you to create a more powerful lesson because you are teaching from an area of great strength. And bonus: it also allows your students to see how their unique skill sets and passions can be vital, invaluable, and applicable for their future.

Ask Yourself:
- Are there any subjects that I am truly passionate about?
- How could I incorporate these passions into my classroom lessons in a meaningful way?

When not drowning under a mountain of marking, I am a passionate person. I get super excited about politics, immigration issues, gender issues, early episodes of *Murder She Wrote,* the sound of aspen trees blowing in the wind, rain, caramel macchiatos, writing, painting, and the feeling after a really good workout. When trying to assess 3,433 assignments, the only thing I feel really passionate about is summer.

If you want to bring passion into the classroom, if you want to create magic in your classroom, if you want to live a creative life, put the assignment book away and have at it. We support you. We encourage you. You will be better for it and so will your students.

Wellness Begets Wellness

One piece of advice that I got as a new mother was, "sleep begets sleep." The idea of letting a newborn skip naps to wear her out does not hold true. Case in point: when travelling to Spain several years ago with my then 9-month-old daughter, she stayed awake for 25 hours straight. Skipping her first naptime (we were probably on our way to the airport) only made her more wired and irritable, which in turn made sleep more difficult to attain, much to the horror of my husband and I and the poor passengers seated around us. Chances are, an infant who has napped well during the day will sleep better through the night. In turn, wellness begets wellness. Putting mental health, physical health, and personal fulfilment at a priority in your life will benefit your students.

A Teacher's Emotions Are Contagious

We have all at one point in time been *that* teacher:

"Michael, sit down."

"Kayla, put away your phone or it's mine."

"Angie, I'm talking. Turn around. When the bell rings I expect everyone in their seats with your books out—excuse me, Anna? You left your BOOK in your LOCKER?!?! Boys and girls, what are you expected to bring into every class? Every. Single. Class!?! Yes, your notebook, a pen, and your book—Sam you left your book at home? AT HOME!? Boys and girls, this is not the type of behavior I expect from you HALFWAY THROUGH THE YEAR."

I have been that teacher, and I can't remember the exact details of why I decided it was a good idea to start the class sounding angry, resentful, and burnt out, but I can tell you two things. First of all, I was not living a very balanced life that week. I was most likely not sleeping enough, not having enough time to myself, not exercising enough, and working way too many hours. This is not the voice of someone who spent an hour at the gym the day before and got eight hours of sleep. Secondly, I can tell you that by the end of the class my students were also feeling angry, resentful, and burnt out. Thanks to me.

Emotions are contagious. We have the power to make students feel calm, uplifted, and focused (or angry, resentful, and burnt out). It runs even further than that. For three years I was the Art teacher at a Science and Technology magnet school in Marietta, Georgia. And for three years I watched students take on the personality and priorities of their elementary teachers. By the end of the school year, Mrs. G.'s students would be a little sassy and confident, but they were also a deeply creative and responsive class. Mrs. T.'s class would be goofy, out in left field. Shoes would be untied and shirts would be untucked, but they were a caring and compassionate group. Mrs. F.'s class would be punctual, neat, and value order, process, and inquiry. They would be confident and up for any new challenge. The first year I saw this happen I chalked it up to coincidence; the second year I was intrigued by it; the third year I would have bet money that it would go that way. If I were the betting type.

A Teacher's Priorities Are Contagious

As my own priorities shifted to wellness, there was an organic and natural shift in my teaching. We moved more. We went outside more. I started considering the needs of my students. When trying (emphasis on trying) to study the Edo period of Japan and the significance of the Haiku, students were restless. Instead of losing my temper with them, I thought about wellness. How long had they been sitting? How much fresh air had they received today? After watching a brief video on Haiku writing, I moved the class outdoors. We spent the rest of the afternoon outside looking at nature and writing Haikus. When on a beautiful spring day my toughest Language Arts class was just not getting into silent reading, we grabbed our jackets and headed outdoors, spread out on the soccer field and read. Their focus and attention were significantly improved after having a short movement break and fresh air.

Emotions are contagious. We have the power to make students feel calm, uplifted, and focused (or angry, resentful, and burnt out).

We talked about the importance of sleep and the need for allocated time away from screens. We talked about stress and stress reduction more. One of the essays in my Grade 8 class was on the effects of social media on teens. Was it an asset or detriment? Students researched and picked a side. We all learned a significant amount about links between screen time and anxiety, obesity, and sleep deprivation. Again, this exploration of wellness was not forced. It was not part of my long-range plan or my personal growth plan. It was a natural occurrence. As wellness became a focus of my life, it spilled over into my classroom. And I would like to think that my students benefited. If we want our students to be healthy, focused, and well-adjusted, we must ourselves be well-adjusted.

Educated Teachers and Students

As you work toward building a better, healthier, more complex life, encourage your students to do the same. Just as a healthy, well-rested teacher is a more effective teacher, the same goes for students. Quality teaching does not occur without wellness. Quality learning cannot occur either. Knowledge of the following key concepts would benefit both teachers and students to know.

Multitasking Does Not Exist

As much as our students (or we ourselves) might not want to believe it, multitasking does not exist. It is actually task shifting. Our brain is wired to focus on one task at a time and it works most effectively when it can focus on a single task for an extended period of time. So when we are juggling multiple tasks, it reduces our productivity and increases the amount of time we have to spend on the one task. As if that were not bad enough, the learning is less flexible so it is not easily applied. This is why texting while studying (or attempting to mark papers) is a horrible idea. The studying will take longer than if a student is focused solely on studying and the learning will not be easily retrieved or applied. As if that were not horrendous enough, as students feel stress while juggling multiple tasks, a stress hormone called cortisol increases, which lessens their ability to remember the information.

Intuitively, I was picking up on this information when I stopped bringing my school work home. With the distractions of family, projects, and household tasks waiting for me at home, I was not able to sit down and focus on one task. Instead, I chose to work at school, after school hours with my classroom door closed (closing the door was key; otherwise, there were too many interruptions). I was able to effectively accomplish a large amount of work in a short period of time.

Sleep Is Essential to Learning (And Teaching!)

I think it is safe to say that most teachers would never dream of teaching under the influence of any type of substance. And yet many of us have arrived at school after a late night of coaching or marking papers with only a few hours of sleep under our belt.

Sleep deprivation causes significant mental impairment. Sleeping only four to five hours per night is equivalent to our blood alcohol level being above the legal driving limit. I have *never* taught a class while under the influence of any substance but I have stayed up numerous times late into the night marking and then gotten up in the early hours of the morning to prepare for a class. I was under the influence of sleep deprivation. This is neither great for us as individuals nor society as a whole. Sleep deprivation can lead to irritability, confusion, depression, cardiovascular disease, obesity, inattention, and concentration difficulties.

Sleep directly affects students' ability to learn as sleep allows for the synthesis of memories. During sleep, our thoughts move from our short-term memory into our long-term memory. The most critical time for memory formation is during the last two hours of sleep. So, if we are not sleeping the full recommended amount (nine to 11 hours for school-aged children, eight to ten hours for teens, seven to eight hours for adults), information is not being transferred into our long-term memory. It does not matter how well we "learn" information. It will not be retained if we are not sleeping. This is just one of the reasons why staying up and cramming the night before a test is simply one of the worst things anyone can do for information retention. Additionally, the social aspect of school can be more challenging for students who are not sleeping. Without enough sleep, willpower decreases and emotional regulation is challenged.

As a teacher, you are probably going to be more prone to distorted thinking and more catastrophizing of things if you are not well-rested. This is why when Abby tosses a wadded-up sheet of paper across the room into the garbage on a day that you are well-rested you might simply, with a wry smile on your face, ask her to please wait until recess to demonstrate her stellar basketball skills. While if Abby takes this action during a week where you are experiencing sleep deprivation, you could very well catastrophize the event, making a far larger issue out of it than need be.

When I am sleep deprived, stressed, and burnt out, I can scarcely remember the names of my students, or where I left my car keys, or what year it is, let alone articulate complex ideas to my students. I do not think I am exaggerating when I say well-rested, healthy teachers would benefit the country as a whole. And on a more micro level, while we may be able to teach the same curriculum or do the same basic lessons regardless of whether we are sleep deprived or not, it is those essential moments with one student in which you will most likely act differently. When you are the significant adult in the life of a very needy (and often very trying) child, your knee-jerk reaction will more likely be that of compassion and understanding if you are well-rested. When you are rested and healthy your response is far more likely to be what you truly want it to be.

Due to changes in our lifestyle and technology, many of us are not getting the sleep that we desperately need to function at optimum levels. If you and your students would like to get more sleep, the first step is to turn off your technology and keep all electronic devices out of the bedroom. Studies have shown that students who are required to turn off their devices and store them outside their bedroom get 42 more minutes of sleep per night—that is 255 hours a year!—than students who do not have any regulation for their devices.

Exercise Is Important

Not only is sleep imperative for learning, but for many of the same reasons, so is exercise. Exercise releases a substance called Brain Derived Neurotropic Factor. (Um. Let's just call it BDNF.)

Basically, BDNF is a fertilizer for the brain and leads to proper memory storage. Greater amounts of BDNF mean that your brain is better equipped to create connections between your brain cells and what you have learned. Additionally, exercise increases the release of the neurotransmitters serotonin, dopamine, and norepinephrine, which are associated with alertness, attentiveness, and mood.

Finally, exercise increases circulation—thus there is more blood in the brain—leading to more glucose, which is brain food.

Looking at this information, it is no coincidence that most of my most creative, inspired classroom ideas came to me when walking in a park or working out. It is also not surprising that when I had one group of students in my class for over two hours (due to scheduling constraints one year, I taught the same group of students for three classes in a row), they were always more focused for the last class when I took them out for a 20-minute run or brisk walk around the soccer field and baseball diamond.

Stress Affects You in Many Ways

For many of us, a certain amount of stress can be a motivating factor, particularly when applied to meeting a deadline or finalizing a project. However, for some, including our students, even small doses of stress can be a paralyzing factor. Teacher and administrator Mark Driedger spent several years researching assessment anxiety. He explains:

> As a former high school teacher, my Grade 12 students were pretty stressed. I started having conversations with those students about their anxiety. I felt it was odd that I didn't have any tools to help them because anxiety is so common for students to have. Teachers have strategies for lots of other things, but I had not talked to many teachers who had strategies for assessment anxiety.

Driedger dove into the research to learn more. One thing that he clarified is that assessment anxiety is about being judged or evaluated. It does not apply only to tests, but also to speeches, projects, written assignments, or anything that is an evaluation. Driedger states:

> It is similar to performance anxiety in that it is the same as how people in society feel when they are judged or evaluated on something. They get anxious to some degree. Every person is different in their ability to cope. Some are more natural with it but the ones that struggle—the ones with higher assessment anxiety—are the ones that don't have coping skills. Mostly because they have not had someone coach them. They have not had any support with it.

I asked Driedger why teachers should care about assessment anxiety. One obvious reason is student wellness. One aspect of stress is that it is transferable. School stress does not remain neatly tucked away at a school and home stress does not live in a vacuum at home. If students have stress in other parts of their life, it is going to get compounded with assessment anxiety. If they have depression, it is compounded with assessment anxiety. If they have issues at home, those issues are compounded with assessment anxiety. In turn, students' anxiety about assessments will make it difficult to cope with other stresses outside the classroom.

This applies to us as well. Consider this scenario. One morning you are on your way to work and you get a flat tire. You are able to pull safely into a service station. What is your response? Most likely you call your school and let them know you will be a bit late and then get the tire fixed and then head into school. Your stress levels might be a bit elevated, but overall you are able to cope with it.

Consider a second scenario. You oversleep. As you are frantically rushing out the door, you spill coffee down the front of your shirt. You rush back inside to change your clothes. Your stress levels are rising. As you are changing, your two sleeping children wake up. When they get out of bed and see that they are leaving, they both start to cry. Your stress levels are rising. You yell for your spouse to get out of the shower to take the kids so you can get out the door. Your stress levels are rising. By the time you make it to your car and drive out of the neighborhood, only to notice that you have a flat tire, you have lost all ability to cope. As you pull into the service station and call your school, you are sobbing hysterically. The rest of the day you are struggling just not to burst into tears.

For some students, that upcoming presentation they have to give in Science class raises their stress levels to the point that when they are faced with any other stresses in their life (the metaphorical flat tire), they simply are unable to cope. Helping students manage their assessment anxiety will positively affect wellness in not just in their school life, but also their social and home life as well.

Secondly, giving our students the tools to cope with assessment anxiety will help them for the duration of their lives. Anxiety will not go away once they graduate school. People who have assessment anxiety in school will tend to have it in other areas of their life. It will carry over to making presentations to their boss or being interviewed for a job. All of these things are an evaluation. Giving our students tools to cope with anxiety will help them for the rest of their life. If you teach students about coping strategies in elementary school, they will transfer.

TOOLS FOR HELPING STUDENTS MANAGE ASSESSMENT ANXIETY

Tool	How It Works
Build confidence.	Students with assessment anxiety need to have their confidence built in a few different places. One of the main areas is *study skills*. We need to teach students about how to study. They can be given information like the following: • Do not cram. Study the content over a period of time rather than just the night before. • Keep your study areas free of distractions. This includes a clean desk with minimal books and papers and the removal of devices such as TVs and cell phones. • Don't study under duress. If you are stressed out and then try to study, your brain will not absorb information in the same way as when you are in a relaxed state. A second area students need to feel confident is with the format of the test. We need to teach students how to approach multiple-choice or true/false tests. Get students comfortable with the test's format. They can be given the following instructions: • Write on the test. Make notes to yourself. You can erase them later if necessary. • Cross out distractors. Focus on what you know to be true. If a student is stressing out over a presentation, get them to present multiple times to a peer or a small group before they present in class. Have them present to you and give them positive feedback. Ensure students feel confident in the format of the assessment as well as in their study skills.
Clarify expectations.	A lot of times anxiety comes with not knowing what to expect in an evaluation. How are they going to be assessed? What parts of the unit are on the test? This is something that needs to be made really clear. If it is a project, show exemplars. Make sure students have access to a detailed rubric from the beginning. Encourage students to self-advocate and to ask for clarification when necessary.

Develop coping strategies.	Coping strategies work well for students who start to show the physical factors of test anxiety. If a student starts to get sweaty palms and an elevated heart rate while taking a test, having coping strategies will help with the physical manifestations of stress. Some possible techniques you can share with students include the following: • Put down the pencil and slowly count backward from ten. • Plant your feet on the ground and feel your feet move around in your shoes. • Try deep breathing techniques or visualization exercises such as imagining yourself in a safe place. • Practice positive self-talk. Basically, you want to get their mind thinking about something other than what is stressing them out.
Discuss physical preparedness.	We need to talk to our students about the importance of eating well, sleeping well, and making sure they plan ahead. It could be a small thing like bringing two sharpened pencils or arriving on time or early for the test.
Watch how you phrase your instructions.	Telling students, "If you take the necessary steps to study, come prepared, and pace yourself, you will do your best," is more effective than saying, "This test is hard; if you don't study you will fail." You ultimately are conveying the same message—you are just framing it in a positive light. For many students, the negative tone will elevate their stress levels and be counter-productive.

Driedger's observation that many teachers do not have the tools or the knowledge to address the mental needs of our students is also being noticed by post-secondary educators. When I spoke with mental health nurse and nursing professor Christine Brownell about anxiety in students, she stated, "There needs to be, very early on, an approach to how we can help these little individuals. We need to help them to understand health and wellness from a holistic perspective." Not only do we need to be talking to our students about sleep, dietary balance, and the physical aspects of wellness, but we must focus on aspects of mental health as well. Brownell states:

> What we find is that in university, we have these amazing, talented young adults that do not have a lot of skills with emotional regulation. That stress—even healthy stress, even motivating stress—can feel toxic to them. I am fascinated that as a post-secondary professor, that in university, I am talking about how to manage stress with students. I am talking about how to emotionally regulate with students. It is not that I am thinking, *Good grief, why didn't you know this earlier?* It is more that I am thinking, *Good grief, why are we not promoting this earlier so that I can then revisit it in post-secondary and polish it, rather than introduce it?*

As teachers, being able to key into our own stressors in life and regulate them is mandatory to our wellness. Likewise, talking to our students about stress and anxiety and coaching them on how to manage it will help them to reach their fullest potential in life.

Wellness Is a Collective Responsibility

Wellness is imperative both to our mastery of teaching as well as for our students to become the most successful learners possible. However, as the goal of this book it to make you healthier, more empowered educators, I must follow this section with a caveat: I am not advocating that it is now the educator's role to ensure that our students get eight to nine hours of sleep, keep their cell phones outside of their bedrooms at night, and eat leafy green vegetables. No, the role of this section is not to put unreasonable and unattainable expectations on teachers. What I am recommending is a culture of wellness in your classroom and schools to cultivate durable learning and metacognition. What I am recommending is that we make our students use their full mental potential by educating them on the mind–body connection.

The more I learned about how our brains work, the more passionate I felt about certain procedures in our classroom that I had before been *laissez-faire* about. Instead of dictating what needed to happen or what students needed to be doing, I explained to them *why* and then asked them to respect my wishes to make them the best students possible. Instead of telling students *what* they should be doing, explain *why*.

LESSONS IN WELLNESS: *WHAT* STUDENTS SHOULD BE DOING AND *WHY*

What	Why
Avoid cramming for a test; rather, study in smaller periods spread out over time.	• Studying in short bursts over a long period of time is effective due to repeated retrieval. The act of forgetting information and then remembering it spread out over time leads to durable learning. Studying for 60 minutes spread out over the course of three days is more effective than studying for 60 minutes the night before a test. • Cramming the night before a test increases anxiety, which leads to the inability to remember and retain information. • Getting a full night's sleep is imperative to moving information from short- to long-term memory.
Put away cell phones and devices and clear desks of everything while writing (or studying in class or taking a self-quiz or a test).	• Multitasking does not exist. • Every time you look at your phone to check a text or to find a new song to listen to, your brain is having to change tasks. • Not only does task shifting completely interrupt your thought process and creative flow, but it also increases your levels of anxiety (which leads to forgetting information) and lowers levels of productivity. That means that you would have to spend *longer* to complete a task while task shifting than someone who was focused on one task at a time.
Get up and go outside to walk three laps around the field.	• Most of us are not getting enough exercise. • The act of exercise releases a brain fertilizer (BDNF) that helps us store memories. • Exercise also releases glucose, which is food to our brain. • Exercise increases our alertness and focus.
Keep all devices outside the bedroom at night.	• Children need eight to 11 hours of sleep per night, depending on their age. • Students who unplug and keep devices outside of their bedroom on average get 42 more minutes of sleep per night. • Lack of sleep leads to depression, cardiovascular disease, obesity, inattention, and concentration difficulties.

Ultimately, it is up to family, friends, community, and students' own self-discipline and determination to create consistent study routines, get enough sleep, and prioritize wellness outside of school. Our job as educators is to provide our students with healthy and stable learning environments and to give them the knowledge and experiences to be the most successful students possible. And at the heart of both is wellness.

We Need Creative Teachers, Students, and Schools

Wellness goes beyond helping teachers and students reach their maximum cognitive abilities. It also affects their creative capabilities—and this is important for both teachers and students. In order for our students to be creative thinkers, they need creative teachers. In order for teachers to be creative individuals, we must have some time and space of our own beyond school. We need this time to partake in our own creative endeavors, but also to decompress and "fill our bucket" so we can go back to teaching feeling refreshed and ready to do the highly creative work required of teachers.

Creativity in Science

Allowing for creativity in Science engages a wider variety of learning abilities. Not all kids are scientists and I understand that. If you allow for creativity, it allows students to focus on what they are interested in. Is it creating a speech, making a video game, creating art? Can you allow for all those things in one Science lesson? Of course you can. It is going to keep those kids engaged. Usually, by Grade 5, I see the spark go away, and it is really sad for me to see that they are not involved. They don't care about school anymore because they have not been creative. A worksheet does not engage kids.

In the future, our students are not just going to need to type in a code to a computer, they are going to need to be creative problem-solvers. The jobs that our students are going to have when they graduate aren't even created yet. Our students will have to think on the fly and be adaptable in all situations. I think that is what gives people an edge in the job market—and in life—to be creative and adaptable and not to just have one singular focus in your life. If that part of the job market crashes, what are you going to do? If students have the creativity, have the foresight to see other opportunities, it will benefit them for sure.
–Sara, Grade 1–12 Teacher

For the Fun of It

In his book *Creativity: Flow and the Psychology of Discovery and Invention*, Mihaly Csikszentmihalyi states, "Creative persons differ from one another in a variety of ways, but in one respect they are unanimous: They all love what they do. It is not the hope of achieving fame or making money that drives them; rather it is the opportunity to do the work that they enjoy doing." Csikszentmihalyi spoke with eminently creative individuals in the fields of science, medicine, engineering, liberal arts, and fine arts, and they all agreed that they do what they do because it is *fun*. Csikszentmihalyi concludes, "So we have to assume that it is not *what* these people do that counts but *how* they do it."

If our perception of teaching through the years becomes tarnished, we are no longer viewing it as fun; therefore, our chances of being highly creative teachers are also diminished—to the detriment of our students and society as a whole.

For many years, I have seen the work and devotion that young first-year teachers pour into their classroom. The creative lesson ideas and the new concepts they invent and implement are nothing short of impressive. And these new teachers love to do it! They talk enthusiastically about a new unit they came up with over the weekend and then later how well it went when implemented. How can we keep that creative spirit going in the classroom for decades? I think the answer is complex, but wellness lies in the heart of it.

If a teacher is resentful of the amount of paperwork she has to do, it is chipping away at her love of teaching. If a teacher feels that the unrealistic demands of teaching are depriving her of time with her own children and family, it is chipping away at her love of teaching. If our perception of teaching through the years becomes tarnished, we are no longer viewing it as fun; therefore, our chances of being highly creative teachers are also diminished—to the detriment of our students and society as a whole. When we make time to reduce our workload and take care of ourselves, we are much more likely in the long run to keep that love of teaching. We are still having fun and able to create magic in our classroom.

"Adventurous Spirits" in the Classroom

Creative teachers are critical to the 21st century—they need to spend less time doing mundane tasks and more time developing their creative spirit. Creativity researcher E. Paul Torrance would agree. Torrance was an Educational Psychology professor at the University of Georgia. He has published more studies on creativity than most of us have written sticky note reminders. Just recently I came across one of his papers on the need for—and lack of—creativity in schools.

Torrance believed that due to the rapid pace in which technology is evolving, it is impossible to know what type of knowledge our students will need in the future. Additionally, students are living in a challenging world with complex issues. They must be trained how to think creatively and problem-solve. A shift must occur from teaching memorization to teaching students how to think. That training requires a radical overhaul of our educational system. At the heart of the change must be creativity. Creativity must be held in high esteem by our schools and be a central part of the curriculum. Creative students must make connections with their creative teachers. According to Torrance, this joining of creative forces is not happening.

Torrance studied two groups of students in multiple elementary schools. The first group tested in the top 20% for IQ. The second group ranked in the top 20% for creativity. While both groups of students performed similarly on achievement tests and reading comprehension tests, the teachers described the students with high IQ as better students, hardworking, ambitious, and studious. The creative group was less known by the teacher and was considered less sociable, less friendly, and less academic by their peers. Torrance's conclusion was that the highly creative child learns just as much as the highly intelligent child without appearing to. In the eyes of many teachers, the child is "doodling" or daydreaming or goofing off, when in reality she is learning.

Torrance said that we need more Mrs. Ellington's, Mr. Davis', Mrs. Delaski's, and Mr. Grunden's in our schools. Okay, he actually said that it is the role of the creative "adventurous-spirited" teacher to create and foster relationships with the highly creative child. "Without creative teachers, creative talent will go unrecognized, undeveloped, and unrewarded. To recruit, supervise, and encourage

We need highly creative
administrators running our schools
and school districts.

creative teachers is the coming responsibility of our school administrators. They face a challenging task."

It *is* the role of administration to hire eminently creative teachers. However, this is a challenge as creative teachers are often not supported by administration. Just as teachers favor the high IQ students over the highly creative ones, school administrators prefer a teacher with a tendency for conformity, and less of a creative nature. Creative teachers can be unpredictable. They are independent thinkers who can become completely absorbed in a task. They challenge the status quo and like to do things in novel and unprecedented manners—often without asking permission. This can be a relative nightmare for the less creative administrator. The solution? According to Torrance, it is that we need highly creative administrators running our schools and school districts. Torrance concluded his study by claiming that humanity's survival depends on fostering creativity in our schools. Pretty passionate words!

While you might not be shocked by the findings in Torrance's study, this might shock you: his paper was published over half a century ago. In 1963 to be exact. It was written in response to "The Space Age!"

Looking through schools in 2018, I still see students' creativity stifled by the less creative teachers, and creative teachers stifled by less creative administrators. Gabbie Stroud, a former teacher in Australia and England and author of *Teacher: One Woman's Struggle to Keep the Heart in Education*, wrote, "I dream of a new paradigm of education, something that isn't a reconstruction of an old industrial model. What we need right now is imagination. We need ingenuity, creativity, and a profound commitment to our teachers, schools, and students." Stroud eventually left the classroom when she simply could not take the restrictions and felt there was no room for creativity due to the constrictions of test taking.

Educator Joy Kirr is still going strong as a classroom teacher but admits that with testing, "It seems as if every year there is something new that teachers must do...The first thing to go is usually creativity. Don't get me wrong, teachers are trying to be creative in giving options to their students, but students themselves don't get much time to show their creativity in classes." Kirr goes on to advocate for creativity, pointing out that students must have a space where they are free to take risks and to solve authentic problems that matter to them. Creativity is paramount to our students today. It is something that teachers must make a priority in their classes.

Fifty-five years after Torrance published his study, we are *still* teaching and testing knowledge over creativity. So, yes, we do need more teachers like Mrs. Ellington. We need creative spirits as educators, principals, and superintendents. I think our first step in accomplishing this feat is fostering our own creative drive. We must become "adventurous-spirited" teachers who advance creativity in our classrooms and inspire our students to be more creative individuals.

Creators of Magic

Recently I had the opportunity to interview former middle school teacher Kath Moors. After teaching for 36 years, Moors retired from education and is now a full-time visual artist. One thing she discussed with me was how to make "magic" happen in our classrooms. In order for that magic to occur, we have to spend time outside of the classroom nurturing our soul. Moors' advice to first-year teachers is that they should start right off prioritizing their health. They should find the time to decompress and to do "whatever feeds your soul." (Although called by a different term, I consider this feeding our soul to be similar to Hildebrand's instruction to fill our bucket and McCreary's insistence that we must take time for self-care. Although all three women have different backgrounds and they term it differently, they agree that we have to do it.)

During our interview, we discussed all aspects of her teaching career. One thing that Moors said that resonated with me was in regard to the toughest part of teaching. According to her, the toughest thing about teaching was all the elements that were *not* part of the classroom teaching: the required assessments, the report cards, the documentation, and various other tedious and mundane tasks. And it was not until she left teaching that she realized how exhausting the imposed paperwork was. Finally, she gave my favorite piece of advice, saying:

Ask Yourself:
- Do I allow myself to spend time with one piece of my students' work? Or do I mark every writing, every quiz, every test?

If I could start my career all over again, I would get on the bandwagon sooner of taking care of myself. It took me a number of years to figure that out. For example, if you have students do a package of 13 poems in a poetry unit, have them select what they believe is a really excellent sampling of their work—one poem. And yes, have them turn in the package of 13 poems but take their one poem and spend time with it.

I used to be the person who would want to read every single sampling of a students' writing. I would mark and analyze every quiz that they wrote. I would assess every test that they took. Do not make the same mistake I did. Instead, look at their work as a progression and take samples that you engage with to mark. Then you are not exhausted, and you are rested. Spend time knowing that child.

When it's all said and done and it's over with—and it's over in a blink of an eye—it's the magic that you have created with kids that's going to be memorable. I have kids from all over the world who write me from social media, who post videos, who come and visit me in my studio and it is not the curriculum that they recall. They recall how we made magic together.

Take care of yourself, or you will not be able to take care of others. Nurture yourself, or you will not be able to create magic in your class.

Moors' advice is immensely wise and at the same time very commonsensical. Take care of yourself, or you will not be able to take care of others. Nurture yourself, or you will not be able to create magic in your class. We do not hear this often enough in education. However, we do hear it every time we board a commercial airplane. I call this premise *The Oxygen Mask Theory*. If you have taken a commercial flight in the past few decades, you know exactly what I mean: "In case of a change in the cabin air pressure, oxygen masks will automatically deploy in the compartment above you. Please remember to secure your own oxygen mask before assisting others."

If you are suffocating, it is going to be awfully hard to offer assistance to others. The same applies to the classroom. If you are too tired, too burnt out, and too deflated to think straight, how are you going to inspire a room full of 32 teenagers? How??? You cannot nurture your soul if you spend every moment outside of school working on school. If you are exhausted on a daily basis the magic will not be present in your classroom.

Ask Yourself:
- What nurtures my soul?
- What depletes me?
- How many minutes a day do I spend doing things that nurture my soul?
- How many minutes a day would I realistically like to spend on myself?

While you are largely in control of your own path towards wellness, it is not a path that you have to—or should—travel on your own. When determining how to cut back on time spent working, consider collaborating with experts in education—other teachers. In the next chapter, we will explore various ways you can start working smarter, not harder with the help of your co-workers.

3

The Benefits of Collaboration

Working Together

The saying, "work smarter, not harder" is easy to classify as trite, or cliché. But *man alive* it is true. Several years ago a guidance counsellor at an open campus high school came and talked to our Grade 7, 8, and 9 students about time management. Because students at that high school work independently and at their own pace, all first-year students are required to take a semester-long time management course. The guidance counsellor elaborated: "Our most successful students admit that they spend more time *planning* an assignment than *completing* it." Her point was that although it is counterintuitive to spend time planning, it saves time in the long run. These students were working smarter, not harder.

At the time I was thinking, *If only my students would take her advice.* Now I think, *If only our teachers would take her advice!*

While collaboration can occur anytime during the year, in order to be most effective, a little upfront planning needs to happen at the start of the school year.

PLANNING FOR THE YEAR

What to Do	Questions to Consider
Establish team members.	• Who are members of my team that I could collaborate with this year? • What are their backgrounds and areas of strength? • How would they complement my areas of strength? • What compromises are going to have to be made?
Organize shared planning time.	• If we are not splitting up our core subjects, do we have shared prep times that could be designated for planning? • Could we have guest teachers come in for half days so that we can work with a consultant to develop our long-range plans together?

Share the accommodations.	• Could I divide up the task of creating accommodated lessons and assessments among my team? • Could one team member provide accommodated material and assessment for one unit and another team member provide accommodated material and assessment for the next, so that I am not having to create my own accommodations for every unit?
Consider logistics.	• If I am going to teach all Grade 4 Science classes, is this something new to the school that we will have to "sell" to parents and admin? Or is this something that is fairly common? • How will grades be entered for elementary students if they have two, three, or four different teachers for their core subjects? (Note: With most grading systems taking place online, this should be easy to set up; however, make sure you check with your admin or office staff to be sure.)
Set up online collaboration.	• If my school is very small and there is only one grade-level teacher, are there district groups that I could join to share ideas and resources? (For example, our district offers online professional development groups for all content areas.)
Establish school and district supports.	• What supports are available to teachers in my district? • Do I have access to educational assistants, diverse learning teachers, curriculum specialists, or consultants? If so, how can I utilize them to the maximum potential? • Would they be willing to team teach with me or help with planning?

Reduce the Number of Classes to Plan For

While secondary Language Arts teachers have it tough in regard to grading, elementary teachers can get slammed with planning. Many elementary teachers in our school district plan for Math, Science, Social Studies, Language Arts, French, Art, Health, and Religion. EVERY DAY. My question is, *WHY?!*

Not only do elementary teachers have to plan a jillion core subjects, but they also have to differentiate and accommodate within each subject. Often significantly. Pass the coffee, I get exhausted just thinking about it.

Which would you rather be responsible for planning, teaching, differentiating for, and assessing for 180 days: one core subject? Or four? By partnering up with a member of your team and dividing up the core subjects, you could cut your daily planning time for core subjects in half! If there are four of you in the same grade level, each teacher could teach one core subject and rotate your classes through. This would cut your planning down for core subjects by 75%! Why is everyone not doing this?

> ### Team Teaching
>
> "I found planning for all eight subjects super overwhelming. Especially if you have all new units starting at the same time. If you have a grade-level team member who you can switch a subject with, even for one year, do it. For a year, it allows you to specialize in the subject that you are teaching twice. So I have switched Math and Science. In that year, I focused on all the Math. I did detailed unit plans and spent my time getting resources for that. She did the same with Science. So for the next year, we had those two subjects covered. I find it works best when you have similar teaching styles and are flexible with your schedules. It reduces your workload big time."
> –Tara, Grade 5 and 6 Teacher

Ask Yourself:
- Who are the members of my team?
- What is one thing that my team members and I could change to work smarter, not harder?
- What initial steps would we have to take to implement this?

Partner up. At the very least, divide the core subjects amongst yourself and another teacher. In an ideal world, you will have a partner who is a lovely person that you love to interact with and you will get to teach your area of expertise and your area of passion. In reality, compromises will have to be made. I don't care if your other grade-level teacher is green, has three heads, and spits fire when angry. Learn to collaborate. You will end up winning by having to plan a fraction of what you would do on your own.

> ### Collaborate with Your Team
>
> In an elementary school setting, there isn't a lot of prep time. Honestly, my time-saving strategy just comes down to being more collaborative with my Grade 6 team—we pass on so many ideas to each other. We have one meeting each week where we discuss Language Arts: What do we need to cover? What does the unit ahead look like? Who has what resources? What resources need to be found or made? How can we divide up the work?
>
> We often have productive meetings because we are all mothers and we are all busy after school. We typically do not stay long anymore because we get the planning done during our collaborative team meetings. So, to save time, I have had to communicate better with my team.
> –Kate, Grade 6 Teacher

Meet the Needs of Your Students

Partnering up does not have to be limited to sharing core classes. If your biggest needs are meeting the needs of a diverse classroom, collaborating with others to meet the needs of your students is beneficial. One particular grade level in our school this year is wildly diverse. There are groups of students who are learning their basic letter sounds while other students are devouring dense chapter books. We have students who do not speak English and students with complex learning and emotional needs. We have students who are refugees and students who have experienced early childhood trauma. We have students who are on the autism spectrum, some who have ADHD, and others with learning disabilities. We also have students who are reading two or more years ahead of their classmates and are frequently bored with the content taught in class. Trying to teach a range of individuals this widely diverse within one contained classroom can be a futile experience.

This wide diversity of students is by no means unique and is, in fact, a snapshot of what is occurring across Canada. This year, teachers in Newfoundland and Labrador are actively speaking out to the press about how our current model of inclusive education is leaving teachers frustrated, angry, and unable to successfully meet the varied needs of their students.

You do not have to meet the needs of your students on your own—collaborate! For example, consider making accommodated lessons and assessment for one topic in Science and sharing it with all of the members of your team. For the next topic, another grade-level teacher makes the accommodated lessons and assessment for all members of the team. Another option is to divide it up by subject area. For example, you create all accommodations and enrichments for Language Arts units, and another grade-level teacher does it for Math units. Exchange all your resources.

Sharing your allocated time with an education assistant or resource teacher will help as well. For example, if the resource teacher is scheduled to work with a handful of students in your class on enrichment projects once a week, instead of working only with your students, see if she would work with all students at your grade level who need enrichment. And likewise, when she is scheduled to go into another grade-level class to help with Math skills later that week, see if she can take the two or three students in your class as well who need Math support. We have tried this model with success in our school—teachers get more support as do the students.

Finally, when making class lists, work carefully with all members of your team to ensure that students are grouped in a way that they will receive the greatest support. For example, if you have two students who are coded "gifted" in Grade 2 and require enrichment and a personalized learning plan, place the two students in the same class. Or if you have three students in Grade 8 who are ELL Level 1 and whose primary language is Spanish, it might be beneficial to have them in the same class. That way when a teacher is researching materials in Spanish or putting together ELL materials, she is meeting the needs of multiple students.

Not only does working smarter, not harder benefit you, it also benefits your students. By working with your team, you are able to meet the increasingly complex social, emotional, and cognitive needs of your students. When we try to do everything in isolation on our own, we exhaust ourselves, and our students' needs are often not being met.

Find a Partner/Mentor

If you are a middle school or high school teacher, your school's schedule might not allow for you to reduce the number of core classes to plan for or to blend your classes based on students' needs. If this is the case, find a partner or mentor in the same grade and subject area that you teach. At the start of the year, request for shared planning time. My first year of teaching Language Arts, I partnered with Ed Yu, who was new to teaching. We were both teaching Grade 7 and 8 Language Arts. We spent evenings and weekends coming up with a long-range plan and planning the scope and sequence of our program. It was a truly collaborative effort. Some days when Yu was full of ideas, he would talk, and I would just listen and type. Other times when I was on a roll with an idea, he would transcribe.

Instead of this...
Instead of trying to be all things to all people (Language Arts teacher, Math teacher, Science teacher, Art specialist, ELL support, gifted coordinator),

Try this...
Find something that interests you and become an expert in it. By collaborating with your team, make it happen. Love teaching Math? Volunteer to teach it to all classes in your grade. Have experience and knowledge in second-language acquisition? Volunteer to take a group of ELL students for intense literacy intervention during a reading period.

Some weeks, when implementing our newly created units, Yu was a few classes ahead of me, and others I was ahead of him. We essentially were each other's guinea pigs. It was not uncommon for one of us to rush into each other's classrooms after trying a new lesson with a warning, "Oh my gosh, it was a disaster! We have to change this!" or a note of triumph, "The kids loved it!"

Having someone to collaborate with, to bounce ideas off of, and to learn from saved huge amounts of time. If I had tried to plan a Grade 7 and 8 program on my own, I would have been frustrated and exhausted. I would have felt isolated. With Yu, planning was an enjoyable time where I was learning from his perspective and building a close co-worker and friend relationship. At the very least, share your ideas with each other.

Studies show that if teachers have mentors, their retention rates in the teaching profession are much higher than for teachers who don't have mentors. Yu and I must have intuitively known that on some level as we became mentors to each other. Only I am not sure who was mentoring whom. I think it changed on a moment to moment basis—sometimes he was challenging my faulty ideas and making recommendations. Other times it was me doing it. Regardless, having someone you can collaborate with is a necessity.

Talk It Out

Collaborating in general just reduces your workload. You can sit down and say, "Okay, let's figure out an approach to this novel study." And you are both researching certain activities to do for it. Start one document. Work jointly on it. Take half an hour one week and hammer it out together. Your unit is now set up now for both of you. You have a direction and you have someone to talk it out with. Having someone to bounce ideas off of makes planning so much more efficient. And you get better ideas because you are collaborating with another like-minded professional. You are brainstorming and pulling from each other's strengths, which results in great lessons. And you did not have to spend hours digging online to find them.

–Tara, Grade 5 and 6 Teacher

Create Interdisciplinary Projects

When planning with your team, consider trying interdisciplinary projects. This could look different depending on your team and the desired outcome. If you teach multiple subjects, creating interdisciplinary projects that students work on in multiple subject areas could save you planning time and give students more time to focus on one project with multiple outcomes. For example, in one of my Grade 8 classes, students wrote an essay on the development of technology since the Renaissance. I used the essay for both a Language Arts grade (assessing the mastery of the writing) and a Social Studies grade (assessing the explanation of the content for understanding). By creating a unit that gives them marks in multiple subjects, students are able to spend more time on that project than they would if they had to create a Language Arts project and a separate Social Studies project.

Another way of integrating content involves creating cross-curricular projects with members of your team. When I was an elementary Art teacher in the United States, I would often brainstorm ideas with our music specialist, Kevin Sanders. We would come up with conceptual art and music themes based on ideas such as "identity," "leadership," or "community." Then once a year we hosted an arts night. Students performed songs, read poetry (I incorporated writing into my art units), and had their art showcased. All work was connected to a common conceptual theme.

Working with Sanders did not necessarily save me hours of marking time but it absolutely contributed to my wellness. Creating cross-curricular units with a talented musician exposed me to musicians and musical concepts that I was not aware of. I was able to bounce ideas around with another artist and receive immediate, honest feedback. Sitting with a like-minded individual and having a conversation was far more creatively fulfilling than staring at a computer screen, writing ideas by myself. Also, throughout teaching the unit, I had someone to check-in with and to ask questions to who had a genuine interest in what was going on in my classroom since we had planned the unit together. Finally, if I had tried to plan and implement the arts night on my own, it would have been nothing short of overwhelming. But with two of us taking it on, it was a feasible, creatively fulfilling project.

If you have a teacher on your team who you enjoy planning with, consider sitting down and creating a cross-curricular unit. Or if you teach multiple subjects to the same group of students, consider creating one project that covers outcomes from a variety of subjects.

A Culture of Collaboration

Having a school culture of collaboration is pretty important to cultivating wellness. Not necessarily collaboration as in you have to collaborate with certain co-workers on a certain day, but rather having a culture where you can at least bounce ideas off of people and share in the load. When you are open to talking about things, you can figure out a quicker way to do something that is taking you forever. Or you can figure out what *not* to do. Or you can simply find justification in what you are already doing. I think that being in a culture that is open to giving and receiving feedback and sharing ideas can save you time and cultivate wellness.
–Mark, Grade 7 and 8 Teacher

Create Projects that Transfer

When planning with your team, consider creating projects that can be used multiple times in a year or throughout multiple grades. For example, when I was teaching Grade 7 and 8 Language Arts, Melissa Thompson, the Grade 9 Language Arts teacher, and I collaborated to develop a daily reading project that we used in Grade 7, 8, and 9 Language Arts. It was a way for students to easily track their reading and create written journal responses. Creating one assignment saved time, since we only developed one template for all three grades. As the students moved up through the grades, they became familiar with the requirements and the assessment of the project. It was a win/win situation. Additionally, because we worked together on creating a project that transferred, it saved us loads of time by dividing up the tasks. Thompson created the charts for students to document what they were reading while I created a rubric for their written response. Then we shared our work with each other. Also, as with the previous integration unit with Sanders, with Thompson I had someone who I could troubleshoot with and check in with regularly about the reading program since she was using the same one with her students. She and I were able to help and support each other throughout the year.

I used the same approach when creating a template for my Grade 7, 8, and 9 poetry slams. Although the content changed (each grade level studied different types of poetry and different poets with the complexity of the poetry increasing every year), the template was the same. After studying different poets or schools of poetry, students wrote, edited, and revised two poems based on that style of poetry. They recited their poems in front of the class, and the class voted on which five candidates would represent them in our poetry slam. My rubric for marking the poems was the same in each grade. While the process was intimidating and new for the Grade 7 students, by the time they reached Grade 9 it was familiar. Additionally, since they had done it previously, the Grade 9 students would create a hype at the approaching unit—they loved rehashing their past experiences and predicting who would be selected for this year's slam. They ultimately felt empowered because they knew the format of the unit.

Creating projects that transfer can work with any subject. Science teacher Rebecca Brewer created a science inquiry project that she uses with her Grade 7, 8, and 9 classes. Students work approximately one day per week on this project in which they have to come up with an area to study, formulate and research three questions, and create an experiment to reinforce the scientific findings from the project. At the end of the year, they present their findings. As they progress through the grades, their projects are expected to grow in complexity and present deeper findings; however, the template remains the same.

Grade 7 and 8 Social Studies teacher Mark Driedger is very intentional with using an assessment template to plug into various curriculum outcomes or grade levels as a time-saving device. In a recent interview, Driedger offered the following information:

I find that when I create types of assessment, I reuse those assessments. So instead of doing a one-off project, I will use the same project and just change it slightly for different units. I am not creating and re-teaching a brand-new thing to do every time. And students get used to the project type, which benefits them. So, I try to keep the medium relatively consistent.

Take something like the Renaissance. Students learn about the Renaissance and all sorts of factors that influenced it like the Black Plague and the demise of the Feudal System. Students have to rank these factors and justify why one is more valuable than the other. Then they have to explain the top three. And then you can either just evaluate their justification of the top three or you can split students into groups after that and they have to debate their top three with each other and come to a consensus about what is the new top one. This way they are listening to other opinions and they are having to justify their own opinion, then think critically and debate together. After the discussion, what does that change about your own top three?

I will probably use the ranking assignments twice within a year. And as a teacher, it saves me time. I can reuse the rubric and reuse the assignment criteria. Plug in your content to a template.

Some teachers are really proud—this is my cool Grade 8 project. And they have a Grade 7 project that is different from that. And a project that is different in Grade 9 when in reality, if it is a well-designed project, they could use the same project in all three grades and change the content. It is still engaging and fun and different. If it is a well-created project, it will transfer.

So whenever possible, avoid doing an assignment just once. Don't spend all this time in class teaching about debate and have the kids just do one debate. It is not fair to the kids. You make them spend all this time on one thing and then make them do it and never get assessed on it again. It is a waste of your time too.

Organize Your Long-Range Plans

Has this ever happened to you?

Upon learning that you will be teaching a new subject or grade level, you grab a flash drive and run around your school begging all the other teachers with experience in your new teaching assignment, "Please, *please, please*, may I have some resources?" And they comply. Because they are nice. And they can see the wild panic in your eyes. Some generous teachers might also let you borrow their enormous three-ring binder with every type of handout you could ever want (along with countless random handouts that you would *never* want). In a moment of relief, you go to the photocopier and for the next two hours carefully reproduce the binders. Ta-da! You have resources.

With the start of the school year in your new position, you have a flash drive and a binder or two bursting with resources and very little time to organize them. You stay after school and work on weekends to throw together lessons that are a hodgepodge of something borrowed and something new. Your class time might look like this: "Get out your reading notebooks! Now it's time for a mini lesson! Now we are working on our vocabulary packets! Pass in your reading logs! What did you learn today—think–pair–share!" Your head spins as you jump from one activity to the next with little cohesion or routine. At the end of the school year, you tell yourself that you *really* need to change some things. However, when summer finally arrives you barely have enough energy for binge-watching the first three seasons of *Sherlock* on Netflix let alone to look critically at your teaching. So you teach the same lessons the following year. And the year after that. And the year after that…because it works well enough.

This is exactly what happened to me. And I know it happens to other teachers because I have countless times sat down with a new teacher and seen the panic in her eyes and said, "Sure, take it!" as I shove my lessons onto her flash drive. In fact, it is such a common occurrence, I have called it the *Flash Drive Phenomenon*. Admittedly it will soon have to change to the *iCloud Phenomenon* or *Google Docs Phenomenon*…Regardless, we all do it. We teach the same hodgepodge of lessons for years without ever stopping in a calm non-panicked manner to look holistically at our assessment—and hence our assignments. And once we do take the time to look at it, they will be one hot mess. For me, my assessments were ineffective, time intensive, and sometimes painfully redundant. And if you are reading this book, I bet at least a handful of yours are too.

Take the time to organize your long-range plans. Single out every assessment and ask yourself two very important questions: "What am I assessing?" and "Is this the best way to assess it?" With every Science lab, every Math quiz, every History worksheet, short-answer test, book report, journal writing, vocabulary handout, and poetry packet you collect to mark, ask yourself those two questions. Once I started, I was ruthless and honest with my purging. And it was worth it. Looking down at the shell that was left of my long-range plans, I felt a thrill. The same thrill I get when seeing my tidy closet with neatly ironed linen shirts or a gleaming kitchen floor free of all dust. I saw order. I saw space. I saw room to breathe. I saw potential to create.

Single out every assessment and ask yourself two very important questions: "What am I assessing?" and "Is this the best way to assess it?"

As you and (hopefully) members of your team get together to plan, please do not underestimate the importance of long-range plans. Since your goal is to create an open, unhurried, and healthy environment for your students to create in (and for you to teach in), you must have a plan to guide you through the year, ensuring that key aspects of the curriculum are covered in meaningful ways. Otherwise, there is bound to be unintentional repetition, omission, and frantic rushing of the content.

Before you sit down to make your long-range plans, let's take a look at how students learn and how the inside of our classroom should look to promote an optimal environment of learning. And that is going to involve some changes in the way we look at learning and changes in the way we run our classroom. If you find the idea of changing your teaching stressful, don't worry. In the chapters that follow, I will take you step-by-step through the process.

Thriving Classrooms

Change the Way You Look at Learning

For years I had the misconception that the more work I assigned, collected, and marked, the better my students learned. I had the misconception that rows of silent students listening to my every word was the pinnacle of an ideal learning environment. I had the misconception that the more grades I had in my gradebook, the better a teacher I was. I was wrong. And it can be backed scientifically.

I know this is highly uncool to say in a time where Bill Nye the Science Guy and Neil deGrasse Tyson are household names, but science might possibly induce panic attacks in me. When people try to explain a complex scientific concept to me I get the same feeling in the pit of my stomach as when I have to do my American taxes: acidic dread. Science is not my ball of wax. But I deeply respect it and think that even crazy Humanities teachers should take a peek at it every once in a while. Especially if it means being more effective with our teaching and reducing our marking time.

The thing I find cool about science is that it has no respect for tradition. It does not disrespect tradition per se, but it is famously known for turning old theories upside down and inside out. So what if science could help us to change the way we looked at learning? What if science could change the way we talk to our students about assignments? And what if all of this could change the way we use our class time? All with the goal to reduce our time spent working outside the classroom and to teach more effectively. Okay, my acidic dread is subsiding a bit now. Let's explore what some scientists are saying about learning.

We have all heard the expression, "You don't have to grade everything you assign." And for years that expression was high on my list of things that irritate me (along with fat-free yogurt and misspelled graffiti). This cliché was usually passed onto me by a well-meaning teacher. I saw this piece of advice as maddening. If I did not mark and return an assignment, what in the world was I supposed to do with it? Start a long-term origami project? Have a bonfire in my den? Open up a papier-mâché studio for children and ironic hipsters? What exactly was I to do with these unmarked assignments??? I saw the idea of not marking everything as trickery—giving your students an assignment and at the last minute being like, "Ha! Just kidding! I am NOT going to grade it. You just did all that work for nothing. Because I am tired and burnt out. And according to this saying that has been circulating the teaching world for decades, I don't have to!" I saw this as a very fast way to lose students' trust. And if you are assessing in the traditional way—where you are the only one in the class allowed to give feedback and students are not given the opportunity for self-reflection—this saying will most likely not work well for you. But if we start to shift the way we look at teaching and learning, this saying works brilliantly. No trickery needed.

Effortful Retrieval

One night, while nodding off on our well-worn leather couch, a metaphorical lightbulb went off and I realized the saying *could* work well for my classroom. And the help came from an unexpected place: cognitive scientists. Those crazy guys.

It was after a long day and I was trudging my way through a fascinating but dense read, *Make It Stick: The Science of Successful Learning* by Peter C. Brown et al. And while I really, *really* was interested in the gist of what the book was saying it was also filled with phrases such as "angular momentum" and "neural pathways". Which I guess is expected from a book with the word "science" in its title. Nevertheless, I was feeling a bit out of my league. Just as I was about to throw in the towel and call it a day, I came across a study that made me sit up attentively and kept me glued to the pages.

One of the key concepts in the book is *effortful retrieval*. Effortful retrieval is the idea that the harder your brain has to work, the better the learning will stick into your memory. For example, reading over notes to study for a quiz is one of the worst ways to study. Although alarmingly it is one of the most commonly used ways by university students. Why is reading over notes one of the worst ways to study? Reading over notes is not only time intensive, but it is easy. It is equivalent to our brain lying on the couch and eating potato chips. Or barbecue kettle chips. Or sweet potato chips, lightly seasoned. Okay, I digress.

Learning is deeper and is retained longer when it's difficult.

Reading over notes is ineffective. And it will not tie things into our memory. Likewise, lecturing to students is a terrible way to review. The brain is not working and therefore the learning will not stick into their long-term memory. In contrast, using flash cards, or dry erase boards, or asking students to write down on a blank sheet of paper what they have learned is a far better way to make the learning stick. Now the brain is having to work to retrieve the information. This is where something important is happening to our neural pathways. Learning is deeper and is retained longer when it's difficult. Although this might feel counterintuitive to students, when learning is easy it does not last. See Effortful Retrieval: How Hard Are Your Students' Brains Working? for metaphorical examples of what does (and does not) promote effortful retrieval in your classroom.

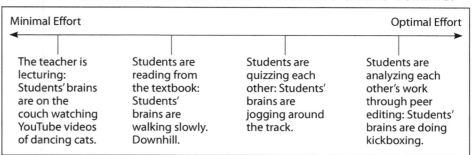

Effortful retrieval and feedback are what students need, not necessarily a grade.

Feedback vs. Grades

The study that made me sit up with interest and continue reading was this: In 2005, a year-and-a-half-long experiment was initiated with a group of Grade 8 students in their Social Studies classes in the United States. Students were given short multiple-choice quizzes on content they had read about but not yet discussed. A second quiz was given at the end of class, once the material had been taught. Finally, a review quiz was given the day before the unit exam. The results were fascinating: At the end of the semester, students scored a full grade higher on a cumulative exam of the material that they had been quizzed on compared to the material that had not been quizzed. In 2007, the study continued. This time it was in Grade 8 Science classes. Again, the results were fascinating: At the end of three semesters, students averaged 79% (C+) on the Science material that had not been previously quizzed, in contrast to 92% (A−) on the material that had been quizzed. Here is the clincher: The quizzes were "no-stakes" quizzes. They were not for a grade. It was not a grade that helped students improve—it was the process of having to retrieve information. Effortful retrieval and feedback are what students need, not necessarily a grade.

At first, I was like, "Wow, that is such valuable information for me to know." And then I was like, "*Seriously!?!* Why has no one told me about this? Shouldn't this be pretty high up on the list of things educators should know!?!" Once I calmed myself down, in time I realized that the saying that irritated me for years, "You don't have to grade everything you assign," is actually true. And backed by scientific evidence nonetheless.

As it turns out, I am not alone in my ignorance of the inner workings of the brain and how to apply it to my students. Effective marking practices in correlation to teacher wellness are not currently being taught in most educational programs, so pre-service teachers are not aware of this going into the field. And teachers like myself who have been in the classroom for decades tend to have not kept up with these new neurological developments. Not surprising since most of us are buried under a pile of assessments.

Giving your students "no-stakes" quizzes or self-quizzes or pre-tests or post-tests that are not for a mark in the gradebook might seem like a waste of time to many teachers and students. However, they could not be more wrong. Giving your students one quiz after a lecture or reading produces stronger learning and remembering than simply reviewing notes or re-reading the content. And you think that pre-tests are a waste of your students' time? Think again. As Brown points out, "Trying to solve a problem before being taught the solution leads to better learning, even when errors are made in the attempt."

"No-Stakes" Quizzes and Assessments

Meaningful learning occurs when students are challenged. Passively listening to a teacher lecture class after class requires little mental recall and therefore results in little learning. Meaningful learning occurs when students are given regular feedback. It does not have to always come in the form of a grade. It took a significant shift in the way I approached learning to become a more effective teacher. And in the process, it significantly reduced the amount of time I spent assessing outside of the classroom.

BENEFITS OF NO-STAKES QUIZZES

Benefit	Why It's Beneficial
Feedback to the teacher	It lets the teacher quickly see how well students know the material so she or he can gauge their teaching accordingly. Half of my class missed questions about theme on a short story self-quiz? I need to go back over the material.
Feedback to students	It helps students to see what they know and what they do not know. I consistently give self-quizzes before my Social Studies tests. If students ace the quiz they have very little work to do to prepare for the test.
Brain workout	The process of trying to remember the information gives students a mental workout (effortful retrieval), which makes the learning stick.

Grades are not essential to the learning process; it is the feedback that is essential.

The no-stakes quiz illustrates to students what they know and what they still need help with. This is key, as students who do not quiz themselves tend to overestimate their grasp of the class material. This self-assessment provides students

Instead of this...
Instead of grading every quiz, pre-test, or handout,

Try this...
Allow students to grade it for themselves. Let them use it as a learning tool for what they know and what they need to work on. As well as giving their brain a hot yoga class.

with a chance to ask for clarification. The quiz is also an example of effortful retrieval. It is giving their brain a workout. As teachers, we have to shift the way we look at learning. For years I felt that grades were intrinsically tied to the learning process when in reality, a good brain workout along with feedback is what our students need. Grades are not essential to the learning process; it is the feedback that is essential.

Morning Meeting

We are always doing formative assessment. I have a meeting every morning. Each morning a different student is in charge of the calendar, so they start by telling me what the date is. And depending on what vocabulary we are covering in Math, they have to tell me if it is an even or an odd date, how to say the date as an ordinal number, and what the expanded form is. I try to determine various levels of understanding like can they skip count forward and backward by this number? And I have a Google form that I complete while the student is doing the calendar, which works as a quick little snapshot of what they are doing and their number sense.
–Jill, Grade 2 Teacher

Below are a few of my favorite methods of no-grade assessment. These are classic methods that you might already know but I find it helpful to have them in one place as a quick reference.

MY FAVORITE NO-GRADE, BRAIN WORKOUT ASSESSMENT ACTIVITIES

Assessment Method	Description
1 or 2, You Decide	If you have extra time in the day, give students a choice as to what they want to work on. For example, students hold up one finger if they want to work on Science or two fingers if they want to work on Social Studies. If the entire class is holding up two fingers, inquire why. Is it because they do not understand the Science assignment? Is it because they like the format better of their Socials project? Have a discussion. This will give you instant feedback into which assignments students prefer and if you follow it up with a conversation, why they prefer them. Because students are having to articulate what type of learning activities they prefer and why, you are challenging them to analyze their own learning preferences. It is a great lesson for them on metacognition.
5 Quick Questions	This works well in Math where memorization of concepts is important. When students come into the classroom, have five quick questions posted on the board for them to complete in their notebooks. Questions should be cumulative in nature, randomly mixed (for maximum effortful retrieval), and cover the core content. Students self-assess.
Graphic Organizers/ Posters	Get students into small groups and spread out across the room. Supply them with chart paper and markers. Have them create graphic organizers to summarize content. For example, they might create a visual timeline of significant events of the Silk Road, the Middle Ages, and the Renaissance or a visual highlighting the elements of the water cycle. Hang posters up along the wall as a visual reminder of the content.
Hands Down, Pencils Up	Instead of asking a question of your class (usually with the result that the same three or four students raise their hand every time), tell your students to grab a piece of scrap paper. Then when you ask the class a question, it is "hands down, pencils up." Everyone needs to take a guess at the answer and write something down. As you walk around the room, ask a student to share a particularly insightful answer. Ideally, it would be a quiet student who might not normally raise her or his hand.

Moving Line/Horseshoe Debate	This works great in getting students up from their desks and talking and moving. Post a controversial statement tied to content. For example, "The age of exploration helped society progress in the 1500s." Students form a spectrum based on their beliefs ranging from strongly agree to strongly disagree. Arrange students into a horseshoe shape so that each student is positioned across from a classmate who holds a different position. Students have to defend their position to someone with an opposing viewpoint. After hearing classmates' ideas and evidence, students can change their position on the spectrum. This not only gets students emotionally tied to the content, but it gives you a quick idea of who has a thorough understanding of what you are studying and who might need more help.
Pre-Test	Give students a pre-test before a unit. Explain to them the reason behind it: effortful retrieval. It gives students an idea of what content they already know, and it gives you an idea of how you need to pace the class. Tired of hearing students say, "That was so easy!" after a particularly challenging unit test, I started to give them pre-tests. Then when I returned their final test grade (usually very high), I stapled their pre-test to it. Then they could see that only a few weeks earlier they only knew 30% or 40% of the content. It reminded them of how far they had come.
Ready, Set, Reveal!	A great concept for Math classes. Give students time to solve a question on individual dry erase boards. Then tell your class, "Ready, set, reveal!" As they hold the dry erase boards up for you to see, you get an immediate gauge of who knows the content and who does not.
Resolving Differing Answers	This can be done as a follow-up to Ready, Set, Reveal! After students solve a Math question on a dry erase board have them get up and find someone with a different answer. The pair has to problem-solve as to who is right and why. This can be applied to any of the core subjects.
Sticky Notes	Using sticky notes works well for a variety of activities. It could be as simple as asking your class to tell you one thing that they learned about today. Students write their answer on a sticky note and post the notes on the board. Students could also write one question they would like answered about the content covered that day and post those as well.
Study Guide from Memory	Before an exam, give students a study guide. This is something that many teachers do already. However, instead of allowing students to look in their notes right away for the answers, for the first half of a class ask students to complete the study guide from memory (no books allowed). This requires effortful retrieval. Treat it almost like a quiz—students clear their desk, and have nothing out but a pen and paper. As you walk around the class, you can see how well your students understand the content. In the second half of the class, students can partner up and help each other fill it in. The process of one student explaining a concept to another is also effortful and therefore helps them embed the concept.
T-Chart	While using T-charts is not a new technique, one Social Studies teacher uses them in a particularly original way. He uses T-charts to get students into the habit of using facts (evidence) to support an opinion. For example, after reading a news story on the refugee crisis, students list five facts they learned (left) and then explain the points of the story that they agree/disagree with (right). Or after reading about the Canadian fur trade, students list five facts about the trade (left) and then analyze how it benefited the inhabitants of Canada (right). This gives the teacher a quick idea of whether students are able to find and identify pertinent facts and then if they are able to apply the facts to support an opinion with one quick glance at their T-chart.
Table of Knowledge/ Carpet of Creativity	As students are working, walk around the room stating, "I am going to circulate, but if you need assistance, go to the table of knowledge." Students can go to a designated table where you can provide them with small-group support. This gives you a quick idea of who needs additional support in the class. Or if there is a larger group they can go to a designated "carpet of creativity." This allows students to assess their own learning needs and decide whether they are capable of doing an assignment independently or whether they require additional support. It also promotes a culture of self-advocacy among students.

Think–Pair–Share	Works great for all grades and all subjects. Instead of asking a question and calling on one student (while the entire class listens passively to their answer), allow students to think for a moment (think) and then turn to a partner and discuss the question (pair). Walk around the room and listen to responses. At the end, ask for volunteers to explain what their partner shared with them (share).
Think–Pair–Square	The same concept as think–pair–share with a slight twist. After sharing ideas with a partner, they pair up with another pair and "square off" their ideas. If they have different ideas, they must discuss and determine who has the correct answer and why.
Ticket-Out-the-Door	Students have to explain a concept or answer a question before they can leave. This works great on sticky notes—they actually have to post their response on the door before they can leave the class.

Socratic Seminar

My favorite form of assessment is a Socratic seminar. A Socratic seminar is based around the whole idea of questioning. For example, we had a Langston Hughes poem versus a Julia Lever piece of prose. Before the seminar, students read each work individually, writing questions down on sticky notes for both the poem and the prose. They then worked in small groups and dissected the works. They discussed the difference between poetry and prose. We were also looking at what imagery and words resonate with them and discussed questions like, "What do you think this means?" and "What are the key differences between these two pieces of work?"

During the seminar, we get out our name tents. We address each other as Mr. Blaufuss or Mrs. Cordell. No first names. We arrange our desks in a circle so we can see everyone. Students have to come with their questions (at least three) and their documentation whether it was their poem or primary source or whatever. And we have our sticky notes with their questions on them. I ask for a volunteer, "Who would like to get the conversations going first? Who would like to start?" And that would lead to people politely agreeing or disagreeing; the questions had to be open-ended.

The Socratic seminar would honestly lead to some of the best conversations about works that we were reading in class: "You know what Mrs. Cordell? I disagree with you. I think that when Langston Hughes wrote this line, he meant that your dreams are…." And then the conversation would just bounce. And the idea is the teacher is just there. She steps in if she needs to but the class carries the conversation. At the end, I would say, "Let's table this conversation. Maybe we will have time for it another time." The entire class would go, "Oh man, no!" like they were excited to talk about Langston Hughes. Students who were initially like, "I don't know what any of this refers to!" they now get it, because the whole class has explained it to them. And it was not me standing in front of the class with my little lecture.

During the seminar, I have my sheet with my students' names and I check if they understand big ideas or what points they make. I am pretty quiet during the whole process. So if I see Ryan in the corner has said nothing, it's because Ryan is either too shy or Ryan has no idea what this is about. So then I have to meet with Ryan separately. This is an excellent way to grasp your students' understanding of the texts without having to do any assessment beyond the classroom.
–Kate, Grade 6 Teacher

Modelling the Growth Process and Authenticity

If you have been teaching and assessing in a traditional manner, chances are your workload looks very similar to mine: Assign a project. Give students time to work on it. Collect it. Assess it. Return it. Assign a new project. Give students time to work on it. Collect it. Assess it. Return it. Assign a new project. Repeat. Repeat. Repeat (three-thousand-four-hundred-and-thirty-three times). Not only is this process exhausting, but it is also teaching our students a completely wrong way to view the learning process.

One Shot at Success?

Psychologist Carol Dweck has devoted 20 years of her life to studying fixed and growth mindsets in individuals. According to Dweck, in the fixed mindset it is essential to be perfect right now. One test—or one assignment—can measure you forever. With a fixed mindset, either you are smart or you are dumb. Either you have it or you don't. Either you are talented or you are not. This type of thinking is powerful. And dangerous. A fixed mindset can be seen in children as young as three years old and it can have a detrimental effect on every aspect of their future life: academic, career, and artistic pursuits as well as their personal relationships. Bullies, for example, tend to have a fixed mindset: "I am superior to you, therefore I have the right to make your life miserable." Moreover, the fixed mindset mentality is simply wrong. Many of the artists, musicians, actresses, athletes, and leaders who we might incorrectly label as "genius" or "gifted" were actually average individuals who were willing to work relentlessly and learn from their mistakes. Photographer Cindy Sherman, one of the most important artists in the 20th century, failed her first photography course. Jackie Joyner-Kersee, arguably the greatest female athlete of all time, finished in last place repeatedly when she started track and field. Joyner-Kersee attributes her success not to inherited ability but rather as a reflection of hour after hour of work.

Teacher and author Starr Sackstein writes that as educators, we must teach students to focus on a growth mindset. Otherwise, growth can come to a screeching halt as students apply labels to themselves such as, "a C student," or "a bad writer," or "not good at public speaking" and then settle into the label, never attempting to surpass it. Moreover, while many students and teachers incorrectly believe that intellectual ability is something largely bestowed on us at birth, cognitive scientists Henry Roediger and Mark McDaniel and storyteller Peter C. Brown explain that this is simply not the case. They explain that the ability to reason, solve, and create is largely within our own control to develop. Understanding this concept is essential as it allows us to see failure as an indication of effort and utilize it as a source for feedback. Students need to understand that when they are doing work of importance, the learning will be difficult. Making mistakes and fixing them is part of developing their ability for advanced learning. Therefore, allowing students to recognize their own weaknesses and giving them time to learn from them and correct them can actually improve their overall intellectual problem-solving ability. Pretty important stuff!

Creating and learning is a process in flux between working, reflecting, and revising…working, reflecting, and revising. And success comes not only to those few students who are "natural writers" or "natural public speakers." An element of success comes to all by reflecting on areas that need improvement and revising accordingly.

Ask Yourself:
- How many opportunities for revision do I give myself when learning a new task before I consider the task "mastered?"
- How many opportunities do I give students to reflect on mistakes and revise accordingly before an assignment is due?
- Does my classroom mirror the "real world" approach to the creative process where an author would have multiple opportunities to revise before publication?

Students' Learning Is Expanded

What never, *ever* happens in real life: You lug home a pile of essays to grade. You spend the evening marking them, paying special attention to Jay's essay. Jay uses many run-on sentences in his essay. You diligently circle every run-on sentence and label it. You even attempt to model for Jay how to correct a sentence or two by inserting proper punctuation. At the end of the essay, you write a clear note to Jay saying, "Jay, in the future, please avoid run-on sentences."

The next day you return the essay to Jay. He looks at your abundance of red ink scrawled across his paper. He reads your comment, "Jay, in the future, please avoid run-on sentences." Jay then throws his hands up in a moment of realization and shouts, "Aha! I get it! After writing run-on sentences for the past six years, I now understand! I am supposed to stop it! Thank you for writing that comment at the bottom of my final paper, which is already graded, when there is nothing I can do about my horrific sentence structure at this point. But I get it! I will never write this way again!" All his sentences from this point on are sheer perfection.

This probably has never happened to you. At least it has never happened to me. Because once the assignment is graded, the learning stops.

So don't collect an assignment for a mark. Collect the assignment and give it back for a writers' workshop. Or peer editing. Or self-editing. Collect the assignment and sit one-on-one with each student and discuss the work with them. Let them return to work on the things you just discussed (this works well for younger students).

Once you decide to exit the never-ending treadmill of collecting an assignment, grading it, returning it, collecting an assignment, grading it, returning it, you will immediately start to notice a change in your students' learning patterns. Specifically, that the learning is expanding. Stretching. Growing. When you delay collecting the assignment—when you curb the urge to take the pile of papers and slap a mark on it —your students benefit.

Once the assignment is graded, the learning stops.

Instead of this...
Instead of assigning a grade and moving on to another assignment,

Try this...
Give your students the opportunity to
1. recognize their mistakes through self-editing/receive feedback on their mistakes;
2. determine how to correct their mistakes; and
3. successfully correct them before you assign a grade.

Repeated Retrieval and Meaningful Content

One year I had the honor of teaching a Grade 9 gifted class that I had also taught in Grade 7 and in Grade 8. The great thing about it was that they were a highly entertaining, charismatic group of kids and we were able to get to know each other inside and out and upside down in those three years. The downside of it that if there were any gaps in their learning in the area of Language Arts before they set off to high school, there was one and only one person to blame: me.

So when I went over an essay-writing assignment with this group of Grade 9 students and then turned to them and said something along the lines of, "Go forth now and write that essay!" I was slightly alarmed when there was an awkward silence in the room as students stared back at me with a look of bewilderment on their face. One brave soul kindly asked me, "Um, Mrs. Bush, can you remind us once again how to write an essay?" Of course I could, but secretly I was puzzled and disappointed—I had taught them how to write an essay in Grade 8. Why, less than a year later, was it completely wiped from their memories? I now strongly suspect the answer lies in the concept of *repeated retrieval*. The idea here is that repeated retrieval or the process of asking students to repeatedly retrieve information that is tied to meaningful content over a span of time allows them to retain it, to be able to retrieve it readily, and to apply it to a variety of situations.

How many times have we given our students a brief lecture on how to write an essay and then asked them to write it? They might retain the information just long enough to write the essay. Then the information slips away. It is probably also the reason that many students arrive in our classes not sure exactly what a subject or a verb or a sentence is for that matter. It might have been covered once in fragmented worksheets in Grade 5 or 6 and then the teacher quickly moved onto something else.

I think the key to repeated retrieval is making students retrieve information tied to meaningful content on multiple occasions. And the meaningful content is key here. We have to change the way we are doing things with our students. We need to make their brain work out, we need to give them regular feedback, and we need to do it multiple times in meaningful ways. And of course, all of this takes class time.

To give you an idea, here is an example of a traditional essay writing assignment not tied to meaningful content versus one that requires students to work harder, retrieve information from memory multiple times, and gives them multiple opportunities for feedback. The first one I call a "Treadmill Assignment" because if this is what your class looks like you are on the never-ending cycle of assigning a lesson, collecting it, and grading it. The second one we will call a "Teaching Well" assignment. Not only are you teaching in a way that supports durable learning, but you have time outside the class to focus on your own wellness and refill your bucket on a daily basis.

The key to repeated retrieval is making students retrieve information tied to meaningful content on multiple occasions.

TREADMILL ASSIGNMENT (PERSUASIVE ESSAY)

- You teach the basic structure of an essay. This is usually delivered in lecture form, possibly with a handout or with notes projected on the SMARTBoard. Students sit passively and listen.
- You assign an essay on an arbitrary topic that has little meaning to most students: e.g., "Should students have to wear uniforms?"
- Students write the essay.
- After writing the essay, students turn it in.
- You put a grade on it and the learning is done.

Time: About 1.5 weeks	Opportunities for improvement: 0	Feedback provided to the student: 1 time (in the form of a grade after the assignment is turned in)

Wellness Note: At the end of a week-and-a-half, you now have to lug home the likely problematic essays and mark them. As well as plan and prepare what to teach next. You have very little time for your own wellness as you are consumed with school work.

There are several things wrong with this picture:

- The content is not meaningful to students.
- There is very little effortful retrieval.
- There is no repeated retrieval.
- In this example, we are modelling to students the fixed mindset. Students have zero opportunities for feedback during the assignment and zero opportunities for growth. We are saying to our students loud and clear, "Either you are a good writer, or you are not. Either you understand essay writing, or you don't." We are clearly supporting the dangerous fixed mindset mentality that our traits are inherent.

- It is not an authentic learning experience. Authentic writing is a process, and much reflection and revision are involved.
- The assignment only covers a handful of learning outcomes: elements of writing and essay writing.

And yet, this traditional essay is how so many of us teach writing; it was how *I* was teaching writing for years. This is just one example of how much of what we are doing as teachers is based on tradition as opposed to research. This tradition of ineffective teaching methods needs to change. So let's consider a second option. One that uses our newfound love of neuroscience!

TEACHING WELL ASSIGNMENT (PERSUASIVE ESSAY)

- Give students time to discuss and generate their own list of five global issues that they are passionate about: e.g., gun control, immigration, the refugee crisis, climate change, gender issues, etc. As they come up with a list, you circulate around the room and discuss with students which one would be a good fit as an essay topic. (**IN-CLASS FEEDBACK!**)
- The next class, you model writing a thesis. Then you give students time to discuss with their peers and figure out a thesis of their own. As they decide on a thesis you walk around the room offering feedback, such as, "This is a great concept, but the thesis may be too broad. How can you narrow it down a bit?" or "This sounds more like a specific detail that you would use to support your thesis. Let's see if we can come up with a more general idea." As students create an appropriate thesis, you initial off on it. Their "ticket-out-the-door" for the class is a thesis that they have discussed with you and that you have initialed. (**IN-CLASS FEEDBACK!**)
- Once they have a solid main idea or thesis, students move on to creating the outline of their essay. As students create their hook and add their supporting details, you walk around the room offering feedback again. As students feel confident with their outline, you initial off. (**IN-CLASS FEEDBACK!**)
- Students spend several classes researching facts for their essay. Going online, or looking through books or articles, they find data to support their thesis. Students summarize key points, recording them on their outline, and document their sources.
- Students move on to writing the essay. At this point, they have received three opportunities for feedback and revision. And three opportunities for growth.
- Toward the end of the writing process, you take a break from writing and give students a self-quiz consisting of a sample essay. They need to identify the hook, thesis, and main supporting ideas. They highlight descriptive words and circle specific details used to support a claim. (**EFFORTFUL RETRIEVAL**)
- Have students self-assess their quiz. As a class, discuss the results. Students see how well they understand the structure of an essay. (**IN-CLASS FEEDBACK!**)
- Once they have completed writing the essay, they are ready to participate in a writers' workshop with two of their peers. They edit the first essay using a peer editing checklist or handout (see How to Give Helpful Feedback (A Humorous Version for Students and Teachers) on page 75 and Peer Editing: Persuasive Essay on pages 76–79). This is a huge brain workout as they are having to recall the structure of an essay, analyze the work, and provide recommendations. (**EFFORTFUL RETRIEVAL**)
- Once students have finished the challenging work of editing the first essay, they edit the second essay. (**EFFORTFUL RETRIEVAL**)
- After they edit their peers' essays, they give feedback and receive feedback on their own essay from two peers. (**IN-CLASS FEEDBACK FROM TWO STUDENTS!**)
- Students revise their essay and turn it in.
- As you mark the essays, highlight one sentence in each essay that is a strong example of using details and persuasive language to prove a point. Put a grade on the essay and return it. (**INDIVIDUAL FEEDBACK**)

- The day you return the essays is a celebration of your students' accomplishments. Ask students to volunteer to read their highlighted sentence to the class. Review with the class their growth, their areas of strength, and what needs to be clarified and improved on. (**WHOLE-CLASS FEEDBACK**)

Time: About 3.5 weeks	Opportunities for improvement: 6	Feedback provided to the student: 8 times (6 during the assignment and 2 at the end of the assignment)
Wellness Note: At the end of three-and-a-half weeks, you take home a pile of polished, revised essays to assess. You have had over three weeks with little to no planning or marking outside of school time.		

In this assignment, students

- received feedback on their topic
- received feedback from you in regard to their thesis
- received feedback from you on their essay outline
- have seen the exemplar on the self-quiz and received feedback from the self-quiz
- have analyzed two different peer essays
- have received feedback from their peers during the writers' workshop
- have demonstrated their competence in a variety of outcomes: research, paraphrasing information, elements of writing, essay writing, analyzing text, and revising text based on feedback

I implemented the above process with my Grade 8 class last year. In December, a few days before winter break, I told students that their first persuasive essay was due. What they did not know was that after the break they would be editing and revising them in a writers' workshop. So as far as my students were concerned, they were submitting their final essay. I collected the essays and sat at my desk, right before the break, looking them over. I quickly scanned the essays as I organized my students into groups for the writers' workshop. As I read them, my heart sank. At one point I closed my eyes and put my head on my desk. There was no denying the truth. These essays were horrible. Don't get me wrong. The students had tried. They just weren't getting it. Paragraphs had no clear topic. Essays had no clear point. Conclusions were outright missing. If I had attempted to mark them at this point, it would have been both labor- and time-intensive. Both the students and I would have felt intense frustration. Instead, I moved forward with my plan for a writers' workshop, knowing that my students would need a significant amount of guidance in editing and whipping these assignments into shape.

After winter break we spent a week-and-a-half in writers' workshops. Working with my students as they edited, I was slightly amused, but mostly sympathetic, as I saw my frustration with the less than stellar papers manifest itself in students as they edited.

"Mrs. Bush, I've read it twice and I can't find the thesis."

Me: "That's because there is no thesis."

"Mrs. Bush, can you please help? I can't find a conclusion."

Me: "Well that makes sense. Since there is NO CONCLUSION! Could you please recommend two to three of the strongest points to be put in a conclusion?"

When I collected the revised essays in January to mark them, it was like they were a different group of essays. They were organized, polished, and convincing.

Every student passed (this certainly would not have been the case with the initial essays I collected in December). And because I was very hands-on during the editing and revision process, they were quick and painless to mark since I was already familiar with the strengths and flaws of my students' essays.

My students learned more from identifying the strengths and flaws in their peers' essays, advising their peers on how to improve, and then finally correcting their own essay than they would have learned from writing three essays. They came out winners and so did I. After all, I did not have to mark three essays—only one!

At the end of this type of project, students should have a durable understanding of concepts such as a thesis and supporting ideas, persuasive language, and detailed facts. This durable knowledge could easily transfer into establishing a structure for a formal class debate or a public speaking assignment. Both require a main idea (thesis) supported by details, and a conclusion arranged in an engaging and convincing manner. You, as a teacher, have covered a slew of learning outcomes.

I share these examples with you to illustrate what effortful retrieval and repeated retrieval tied to meaningful content may look like in your classroom. The same could be applied easily to a Social Studies essay, an Art assignment, or a Science inquiry project. This is by no means meant as THE WAY to teach essay writing or THE WAY to teach anything for that matter. Create a process that works for you and the needs of your students. Just please remember to give students lots of feedback and opportunities for growth. And put their minds to work!

Not only does repeated retrieval tied to meaningful content help students to attain durable understanding but it transfers the work onto the students. Students are not passively listening to lectures or reading from textbooks—they are challenged. Students are working harder than the teacher—and that is how a thriving classroom should look.

Testing Structures

We took about eight weeks to complete our Grade 3 structures unit. It was constant testing and revision. We looked at the "Three Little Pigs" story. We read the story and I left out the last page so students did not know what happens in my version of the book. Students had to write their own ending.

Then students had to build their first house out of paperclips, pipe cleaners, and drinking straws. And it was frustrating. With a partner, they drew up what they thought their magical house would look like and it didn't work out that way because the materials did not work that way. Then they had to revise their blueprints and keep testing. And then they had an end date—the test date—with the big bad wolf (which was a hair dryer). And we would test, "Is your house going to fall over or not?" We had fun with it. We took before and after pictures and slow-motion video.

And the next structure was a stick house. They worked individually on this one. They made the house smaller and they used graph paper to plan it. After each build, they had to provide details such as, "My structure works well when I use X" or "Does my structure look exactly the same as my first blueprint?" and "Why did it turn out the way it did?" For testing in the second round we ended up using an air compressor.

> And for the last build they used bricks made from modelling clay. There is a lot of revision that goes along with the unit. And at Grade 3 they are very able to assess their structures and what is going to work and what's not. It's really frustrating for those kids who are used to getting it right the first time and who can answer all the answers in class, but when it comes to building things, it requires a lot of trial and error, and a lot of revision.
> –Sara, Grade 1–12 Teacher

How to Learn vs. The Need to Learn

Like most brilliant teaching moments in my classroom, this one happened totally by accident. It was the day before the first test of the year and I was talking to students about study skills. Unsuccessfully.

"So…what do you do to prepare for a test?"

Twenty-nine blank stares back at me.

"How about flash cards?"

More blank stares.

"Raise your hand if you actually know what I am talking about when I say *flash cards*."

Three students nervously raised their hand and looked around guiltily.

I decided that it was time I talked to my students about learning. Every year, students are taking on more and more responsibility in school. Taking accountability for their learning is a natural expectation for teachers to have for all students. But how can they learn if they don't know how? And how will they learn if we have never taught them how? So, I talked to them about making their brains workout while studying and the importance of effortful and repeated retrieval. I postponed the test and instead we spent one class cutting up sheets of paper and making flash cards and the next class using the flash cards. Again, more time was needed. But again, it was time well spent. We must talk to our students not only about *why* they should learn the content in our classes but also *how* they can learn the content in our classes. Teacher, author, scholar, and social advocate Linda Lyman explains: "Introduce students of any age to metacognition, to how their brains work, and their learning will increase. Teach them that intelligence is not fixed, that the brain changes every day in response to experience and effort."

Ultimately, after I began having a discussion with my students about how we learn, we all realized that as a class, it was not the grade that made them more knowledgeable, it was the process of retrieving the information and the process of receiving feedback on what they know and did not know. In *Hacking Assessment*, Starr Sackstein writes, "Traditional grading language is passive and is often negative, so we can shift the way we talk about assessment. Instead of using the words 'grade' or 'grading,' use 'assessment' or 'assessing.' We must be conscious of our diction, as our words characterize our thinking and communicate attitude: One simple word change can affect the connotation drastically." So, when a student asks, "Mrs. Bush, is this for a grade?" I can say, "No, it is our way of assessing what you know already and what you need help with."

After talking with students, I realized that no, we do not have to mark everything we assign. And I can be honest and upfront with my students. And they are okay with it. In fact, as long as I treat a pre-test or a self-quiz seriously, my classes take them just as seriously as they would a graded assessment. During self-

We must talk to our students not only about why *they should learn the content in our classes but also* how *they can learn the content in our classes.*

assessments, I ask students to clear everything off their desk. Their cell phones are put away. The class is silent until the last person finishes. I walk around the room, monitoring. I give them ample time to complete the assessment to illustrate this is not busywork or something to be rushed through. They will follow your attitude. Stress the importance of this activity. I always tell my students that this will help them save time at home. I explain to my students, "Why study something that you already know? Instead, focus on the very specific areas that you need help with. Don't worry if you do not know the answer. Remember: you are giving your brain a workout. It is not supposed to be easy."

Once you begin to teach your students how we learn, students realize

- the benefits of taking a self-quiz
- the importance of taking a pre-test/post-test
- the importance of making their brain work out
- the importance of repeatedly making their brain work
- that this is about the learning NOT the marking
- that learning changes the physical aspect of their brain
- that intelligence is not a fixed trait

Authentic Learning Takes Time

The night before my book was due to my publisher, I sat down and said to myself, "I better type up something." And so while listening to Adele and texting, I sat down and churned this out.

Just kidding. I did not have a publisher at the time I was writing the content of this chapter. And it took years of research, editing, and revision to get this book to completion. And texting completely stresses me out and I avoid it at all costs as a means of communication.

The point being, if most of us would not think of writing a business letter, or a letter of recommendation, or an official work e-mail without several rounds of editing, why do we allow our students to turn in work without first requiring them to edit and revise? This is not applicable only to written work; it absolutely applies to projects, debates, presentations, and public speaking.

Just ask Carmine Gallo, former news correspondent, marketing guru, and author. According to Gallo, when it comes to public speaking, it takes practice to appear natural. Hours and hours and hours of practice (Gallo is obviously in agreement with Dweck in regard to the power of the growth mindset). According to Gallo, the only way for speakers to appear natural is through relentless practice. In fact, the best presentations he has seen took *hundreds of hours* to perfect. One 20-minute presentation he saw at Apple required 250 hours of preparation. An imperative part of practice is receiving feedback at all stages of the presentation. The best public speakers in the world were not great speakers to begin with; they were simply great at practicing and revising.

For years I asked my students to do presentations and I always begged them to go home and practice. But I never required it. I never allocated class time for it. By not giving students in-class time to practice, receive feedback, and revise, I was diminishing the importance of the revision process. It was only in the past few years that I required them to practice and revise their presentation a minimum of two times before I would even let them stand up and present (they could practice and revise up to four times for bonus marks) and I gave them a week of class time to practice, receive feedback, revise, practice again, receive feedback and revise (see Public Speaking Unit – Preparation on page 80). The result was astonishing. They were by far the best set of presentations across the board that I have seen in my teaching career.

When we provide class time for our students to practice their opening speech multiple times before a debate, they will know to practice sample questions before an interview. When we provide class time for students to revise a story multiple times before submitting it, we are demonstrating to them the importance of a carefully written scholarship application. Or a carefully written cover letter. We are preparing our students for life beyond our classroom walls.

Now let's take a moment to tie this back to wellness. How does the Teaching Well model apply to your own life? How does it help to facilitate your own wellness? To give you a visual, let's look at a timeline of ten weeks of teaching. In the Treadmill model, you are collecting and grading assignments every one-and-a-half weeks. Additionally, you are having to plan new lessons and forms of assessment constantly. This model would have you working long days with little time for your own life. This offers you very little time to take care of your own physical and mental health.

In the Teaching Well model, while you are consistently conducting formative assessment with your class and offering ongoing in-class feedback, you are taking home assignments to mark once every three-and-a-half weeks. These assessments allow for growth and cover a wide variety of outcomes. It might take time and practice to switch from the more traditional way of "treadmill" marking to "wellness" marking. Go slowly and ease yourself into it. In time, I think we can all agree that extending the time you allow students to work on assignments will also impact your own wellness in a significant way.

TREADMILL ASSIGNMENTS (TEN WEEKS)

Collect/Mark Assignments	Collect/Mark Assignments	Collect/Mark Assignments	Collect/Mark Assignments	Collect/Mark Assignments	Collect/Mark Assignments				
September				October				November	
Week 1	Week 2	Week 3	Week 4	Week 1	Week 2	Week 3	Week 4	Week 1	Week 2

TEACHING WELL ASSIGNMENTS (TEN WEEKS)

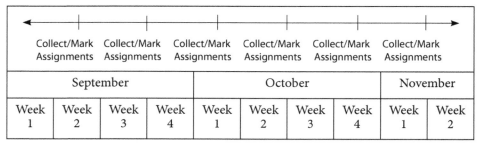

In-class feedback	Collect/Mark Assignments	In-class feedback	Collect/Mark Assignments	In-class feedback					
September				October				November	
Week 1	Week 2	Week 3	Week 4	Week 1	Week 2	Week 3	Week 4	Week 1	Week 2

Guidelines for Minimizing and Rebuilding Assignments

If you are currently thinking, *Okay, preparing our students for life beyond our classroom sounds great, Lisa, now how in the heck do I do it?*, continue reading as the following pages offer a few guidelines for cleaning out your assignments and getting rid of a whole lot of unnecessary items. This will give your students more time to think critically, learn in an authentic manner, and reduce your marking drastically.

But wait. Before you sit down and say, "Let's do this!" let me just interject one note of caution. If you are looking for dramatic results, cleaning out your lessons works best when done in one big swoop. If you desperately want to reduce your marking, do it all at once. This process does take a bit of time. Please do not sit down at 9:00 pm on a Tuesday night after a long day of teaching with a heaping glass of wine in your hand and think to yourself, *I'm so tired I cannot think straight, and I am being evaluated at 8:30 am tomorrow, but what the heck? Let's get this done.* You will need plenty of time. And in the words of Hercule Poirot, you will need *the little grey cells.* Pick a time when you have energy, focus, and are not rushed. Cleaning out your long-range plans takes time initially, but I promise you the results are worth your effort. You will save countless hours of planning and marking once the school year gets underway.

When purging your lessons, be fearless. When I first cut my long-range plans, I was worried I would run out of things to teach. The opposite was true. When I gave my students time to reflect on, edit, and revise their work, read independently, and write regularly in journals, as the school year progressed, I realized I *still* had too much stuff. Several times during the year I had to cut out additional non-essential lessons. So, if you are looking down at a nearly empty long-range plan and saying to yourself, *Great Lisa! I have nothing to teach, now what?* Do not panic. Focus on the basic authentic lessons and give your students plenty of time for the creation process.

Ask Yourself:
- What assignments or activities do I remember fondly from my time as a student?

Chances are, if you still can remember something years or decades later, it was a novel or emotionally engaging assignment that you connected with on a personal level. Think of the things you loved the most and use these memories to inspire your rebuilding of teaching. Conversely, think of the things you despised in your classes and determine how to not fall into the same erroneous patterns of teaching.

TEN TIPS FOR MINIMIZING AND REBUILDING LESSONS

Tip	Description	Rationale
1. Detach yourself from tradition.	Eliminate assignments that you have used for many years but offer little value.	Often we require our students to do book reports or novel studies or bell work or reading logs not because it is the best practice supported by research but simply because that was the way it has been done for decades. This type of mentality is not only unproductive, but it is also harmful to our students' education. Ditch the assignments that you teach simply because you have always taught something that way.
2. Detach yourself from personal bias.	Stop teaching lessons simply because you like them. Take an impartial look at the purpose and effectiveness of the lesson.	While it is important for us to bring our passions into our classroom and incorporate them into our assignments in meaningful ways, teaching a lesson just because we think it is *super fun!* is not the way to go (after all, your idea of fun and a student's idea of fun most likely differ). When cleaning out your teaching, remove sentiment from the picture. Avoid telling yourself, *Well this Science handout was created three decades ago and is completely formulaic, but it is about bees! And bees are fantastic!*

3. Remove assignments that do not allow depth of thought.	Get rid of assignments that require rote memorization of insignificant facts with no opportunity for higher-level thinking. These assignments usually require one uniform response and give students no room for exploring their own interests.	How do your students feel sitting and completing prefabricated packets about the origin of Thanksgiving? Or answering Social Studies questions at the end of every section in the book. Bored? Disengaged? Resentful? Yup. And can you blame them? I certainly can't. Whenever possible, get rid of assignments that do not allow students to connect facts with meaningful concepts or use their higher-level thinking skills.
4. Remove assessments that are fragmented.	Students learn best when they can spend a considerable amount of time looking deeply into a concept. Concepts and facts should be tied together.	We throw at our students a reading comprehension test with outdated material because we want to see what level they are reading. Then we require them to write a business letter to a fictional small appliance company about a faulty hairdryer because that is what they will be tested on at the end of the year. Finally, we throw grammar handouts at them that are completely unrelated to anything we are reading or writing in class. No wonder so many students hate school! This type of fragmented work is not only uninspiring, but it is shallow and an ineffective way of teaching. The likelihood that students will retain this information is scarce. Lessons that are taught in isolation and are not connected to a bigger unit or concept should be revised.
5. Remove assignments that are ineffective.	Remove assignments that are not effective at creating durable, long-lasting understanding of concepts.	Are you using your class time ineffectively by having your students sit passively at their desks and listen to you lecture for an upcoming test? Are your students sitting passively at their desks on a regular basis listening to classmates' speeches or book reports? You will need to change or eliminate assignments that are an ineffective use of class time.
6. Focus on the essentials.	Focus on the key elements that you want your students to take from your class. Get rid of everything else.	Think about what skills are essential for your students to master when they leave your classroom: e.g., critical thinking, problem-solving, reading comprehension, research skills. Make these the pillars of your teaching and get rid of the frills that serve as a distraction. Eliminating the frills will also cut back on your paperwork and allow students more time with meaningful assignments.
7. Focus on depth as opposed to breadth.	Avoid trying to race through every detail of the content. Allow your students to spend time exploring the pillars of the curriculum.	It is critical to allow space and time for students to delve deeply within a subject. Durable learning takes both time and effort. Otherwise, the learning does not stick. Sure, students might retain the information for a test or quiz or paper but after that, it is *goodbye* to the information. Therefore, teachers who want their students to experience deep learning while trying to cram a huge amount of material into their brains as quickly as possible are attempting a task as futile as attempting to put me on diet. Or a budget. It just ain't gonna work out well.

8. Allow for assignments that cover numerous objectives.	Create assignments that allow you to assess numerous learning outcomes.	Do you have to assess your students' research skills as well as their competency in essay writing? Instead of assigning a research paper AND an essay, assign a persuasive essay that requires research. Do you have to teach figurative language and short stories? Instead of assigning a handout on figurative language AND a short story writing assignment, assign a short story that incorporates descriptive writing and figurative language. In order for your students to have more time to work on their assignments, they should cover a whole boatload of objectives. The more objectives that an assignment covers, the more time your students can spend on that one assignment. By also covering numerous objectives with one assignment, you are drastically reducing the time you spend planning and assessing.
9. Allow for student choice and expression.	Students should be able to have room for creativity and choice within an assignment.	Give students guidelines but also give them room to explore within those parameters. In a class where all students are covering the same objectives in an assignment (e.g., understanding the factors that shaped the age of exploration) give them the opportunity to approach it in different ways. Some students might study technological advances of ship-building and create a three-dimensional model of one of the ships frequently used for overseas voyages. Other students might research the life of an explorer and create journal entries and a map that documents his voyage. With technology becoming more affordable and accessible in schools, it is easy to let students select the particular content that they research and develop.
10. Allow structured time for students to reflect, explore, and revise.	Give students ample time in class for reflection and revision. However, make sure that they have mini deadlines that are clearly posted to help them focus their time.	Fight the urge to try to rush your students through an assignment. Remember, you do not want to give your students the message that a polished speech, or project, or piece of writing is something that should be done in one fell swoop. However, at the same time, avoid giving students a large amount of time with few guidelines. This can be overwhelming even for the most mature and organized students. And for those students who struggle with time management and organization, lack of structure can be disastrous. At the beginning of each assignment, review the project in its entirety with your class. If possible, post mini deadlines in-class or online and have students enter them in their agendas or phones as reminders. Allow plenty of time for students to study the rubric and exemplars, brainstorm ideas, create an outline, research, work, receive and give feedback, revise, and possibly edit and revise again. Post a final deadline with multiple mini deadlines leading up to it. Students will not be rushed but at the same time, they will have an understanding that they need to be focused each day on a specific task in order to complete the assignment. It will dispel the all too common tendency for students to say, "Oh wow, I have a month until my story is due, I have so much time…I can slack today." If they see that their outline must be approved tomorrow and their rough draft is due a few days after that, they will be far less likely to procrastinate and be far more aware of the importance of efficient time management.

> ## Dropping Word Study
>
> Something that I used to teach in third grade and then fifth grade was word study. Which is just like, "We no longer really teach spelling, so we are going to do word study instead." And I was always just like, "What the flip is word study? How is that different from spelling?" But I went along with it. I did this whole word study *Tic Tac Know* and *Choice Board Three in a Row* activities that were really quite lame. I carried it with me for a couple of years and made minor changes. I didn't learn anything about my students. I didn't have time to correct it all because it was coming in every week. I would get all their notebooks and think, this is just regurgitation. They are not learning anything from this. And this has effectively ruined three years of my life! So why am I doing this? I wasn't consistent with collecting it so they could get away with not doing it. I took a PD this summer on word study. And they showed me different ways to incorporate it into our units through discussion. So it was meaningful and relevant and not just something else to mark.
>
> The one thing that I did take away from my master's degree is if it is not an authentic problem—if it is not based in the real world—then you shouldn't be teaching it. If it has no connection to the real world the kids will be bored and will not get anything from it. And I'm still working on it. Still, to this day, I'm working on it.
>
> –Kate, Grade 6 Teacher

Ask Yourself:
- What will my students remember from my class when they are 40?

Some of my favorite projects allow for both student choice, authenticity, and cover a wide range of objectives.

AUTHENTIC ASSIGNMENTS FOR THE 21ST CENTURY

Assignment	Description
Podcast	Students create a two- to three-minute instructional podcast on an individual topic of choice. Topics could include how to build a lunar space module, ten snowboarding tips for newbies, five things you need to know to get hired at Google, etc.
Video Interview	Working in pairs, students write and film a three-minute interview with someone they believe played an important role in their field. One student will be the interviewer while the other will be the interviewee. Interview subjects could include scientists, mathematicians, writers, civil rights activists, musicians, pop-culture icons, politicians, religious figures, athletes, etc.
Video	Students create a 60-second movie trailer for their favorite book of all time. For students in younger grades, this could be a simple cell phone video of them describing the merits of the book.
Blog	Students create a series of nonfiction blog posts on a topic of their choosing. This is a great project to allow students to work on at intervals throughout the year. While it depends on how much class time students are allocated, they could create six or more polished blog posts in one year.
Historical Blog	Students create a blog written as a significant historical figure. From a first-person point of view, they chronical that person's experiences through a historical event in five to six blog posts.

Far-Reaching Benefits

The benefits of minimizing your assignments are far-reaching. If you previously taught a hodgepodge of fragmented lessons or required students to churn out assignments at breakneck speed, you will now notice that your students are not in a constant state of panic. They are calmer and less stressed. Students lose fewer assignments. They will have an easier time keeping up with the pace of the class. Since you are now taking your time with one assignment, spending several weeks on one paper or one presentation, and spending plenty of time in class editing and revising, you will also notice a decrease in late or missing assignments.

There will be multiple benefits for you as well. You will no longer have to hunt students down for missing handouts or worksheets. Previously it was the norm for me to chase down three dozen students for miscellaneous missing assignments at the end of each term when progress reports were due. And many of these assignments were so small and insignificant that when I shrieked, "Anna, where is vocabulary handout 6.2 from this past February?!" her reply was, "Huh? What handout?" In other words, the assignment was so insignificant that the student had no memory of it. This will come to an end with minimizing your lessons.

Since your collection of papers and electronic assignments is now fairly minimal, you will also notice the time spent having to organize papers or electronic files will decrease. The likelihood of your entering an incorrect grade and then having to go back and fix it will decrease. Your classroom will contain fewer papers and therefore you will not have to spend as much time tidying up at the end of each day. In a world where we have an ever-increasing amount of stuff, less is truly more. You will begin to notice these numerous benefits when streamlining your teaching assignments.

Having clear long-range plans and daily lesson plans will help to support your new approach to teaching with administrators and parents. If, for whatever reason, you are apprehensive about how your administration will respond to fewer grades in your gradebook, I recommend that you schedule a time to sit down with them for a discussion. Explain the benefits of allowing students more time with assignments. Explain the benefits of getting rid of non-essential and ineffective assignments. Explain that students are actually receiving *more* feedback than previously and are extending their learning even though they have fewer grades in the gradebook. In my case, my administration was supportive from the beginning, but I was not sure how the parents would respond. I wanted to be proactive, so I posted on my class website what students were doing in my class on a weekly basis. Parents could go online and get a very clear idea of the work that was being done in my class at any given point in time. I did not have any issues from parents about the amount of assessment in my class, and I hope that your experience will be equally as positive.

Do They Want to Be Here?

At the end of it, sometimes the focus is too much on the assessment piece and the paperwork. We should look at the root of it. We should be asking, "Are they enjoying school? Do they want to be here? Do they enjoy spending seven hours a day with me? Or are they hating coming to school every day and it is now a struggle at home just to get them out the door?" That to me is more concerning than, "Do I have enough marks in my gradebook?"

–Tara, Grade 5 and 6 Teacher

Fear of Change

After basking in the delight of thinking I could significantly reduce my workload, I did what I do best: Worry. Now I hate to brag, but if there is one thing that I excel in, it is thinking about every possible problematic scenario that could occur in any given hypothetical situation and worry incessantly about it. And so, worry about changing my assessment method—and therefore my teaching methods—I did. However, overriding my worry was my early-pregnancy exhaustion. So that year I gradually implemented a few changes to my teaching approach. A few of my most pressing concerns included:

1. If my students are not bombarded with constant due dates, will they start to slack off?
2. If I ask my students to complete assignments that are not graded, will they still take the assignment seriously?
3. If I mark less, will my students learn less?

As it turns out, the answers were *no*, *yes*, and *absolutely not*.

As I started to grade less, I noticed several surprising shifts in my students' actions that were diametrically opposed to the behavior I had initially predicted (just another example of how worrying is a big fat waste of energy). My students were engaged in the classroom. They were more challenged than in previous years. Their writing/critical thinking/public speaking was significantly

Ask Yourself:
- What concerns do I have about dramatically changing my marking load? Pushback from administration? Or parents? The work initially involved in changing my teaching? The fear that it will not work with my students in my classroom?

Make a list of concerns that might be holding you back from following through on reducing your workload. Next to each concern, list some possible solutions. Or even better yet, discuss these concerns and solutions with a supportive colleague.

improving. They were working harder. They had more ownership. My classroom became more student-centred.

Until you do it for yourself and see the positive results the concept can be terrifying. Ultimately, by marking less, we are doing two acts that are simultaneously terrifying and best practices in teaching. We are

1. giving up an element of control of our class; and
2. creating student-centred environments.

....

The Courage to Ask a Question

If a student doesn't understand one curriculum outcome it's not the greatest of my concerns. Instead, I focus on whether they are learning how to learn. Are they learning how to find information? Or how to problem-solve? Or ask for help? Some kids, I just want to find the courage to ask a question. I just want them to get to the point where they are confident enough to ask for help.
–Vanessa, Grade 5 Teacher

....

Letting Go of Control

Language Arts teacher and writer Pernille Ripp does not mince words when it comes to control. In her opinion, education—and educators—are gaga over control. Though we try to mask it through euphemisms such as "manage," "supervise," or "facilitate," what we are really talking about is control. Specifically, our control in the classroom and our control over our students.

My three-year-old daughter has done an excellent job of reprogramming the way I view control. When we go for walks at our provincial park and I am in control, we get in a very brisk 45-minute walk. There is much hurrying along and keeping her "focused" and on the path. Threats are mingled with bribes, "If you don't hurry, we will not have time for the playground." There is very little unpredictability in the routine and very little learning. When I release control (usually when it is a beautiful day and I do not want to return indoors), I let her lead. We study spider webs for 20 minutes. We greet every cyclist and stop to talk with every dog owner and puppy who are willing. We drop pebbles off a bridge for eons. An older couple stops to help us gather rocks. We study seed pods. We search for ladybugs and chase grasshoppers through the wildflowers. When I release control over the path of the walk and the tight time frame it has to occur in, wondrous things happen. The same 45-minute walk now takes two hours. But it is a magical two hours. Deep learning occurs without threats or bribes.

If you are petrified of giving up control, you are in good company. Even master teachers like Ripp can be petrified to give over control in her classroom. She had a vision of her students turning into "wild things, barely contained within the walls." And yet she noted that once she had the courage to transition *my classroom* to *our classroom*, where students decided everything from furniture arrangements to the structure of the projects, the opposite occurred. When she handed over the reins to her students, "far from staging *Lord of the Flies*, they collaborated and supported each other. Our room seemed to sigh with satisfaction and begin to relax."

Allow Students to Become the "Experts"

By allowing students to look at exemplars and decide for themselves what qualifies as quality elements of work, you are no longer the only expert in the room. There are now 28 or 32 other individuals with an opinion that deserves to be heard. Also, by having students assess each other's work, we are no longer the sole individual in the room allowed to point out the flaws and merits in students' work. Distributing the work among all members of the class (not just the teacher) is a far more brilliant use of everyone's time but it is also slightly terrifying. Educator Starr Sackstein points out, "When there is only one person in the room capable of providing useful feedback, there is no way every child will get what he or she needs all of the time….Serious educational consequences result when teachers dominate the feedback loop." When we engage our students in peer editing, we are able to capitalize on the varied expertise of our students, we are finding a solution to the imbalanced ratio of one teacher to many learners, and we are creating independent learners. Great things happen when we give up control.

Student-Centred Classrooms

By allowing students to become the experts and to be the ones involved in the assessment, feedback, and revision loop, our classrooms will naturally become a student-centred environments. Students are editing in partners or in small groups or working individually while I have the opportunity to work one-on-one conferencing with other students.

Gone are the days where I am pacing the classroom floor lecturing on what elements make a quality project or reminding students, "Fifteen minutes left until your assignments are due!" and "Stay on the path!" and "No time to look for ladybugs today!" Now my students set the tone and the pace of the class. I instead check in with them, "Do you need half a class to finish? A whole class? Three classes?" (This actually tends to happen as I grossly underestimate the time needed for deep learning to occur.)

If you have been using the traditional way of marking, class time is going to look a little bit different. For the most part, you will be working *with* students. Sitting with them. Mentoring them. Providing them with feedback and guidance

Fill as much meaningful, individualized feedback into a class as possible. This will eliminate hours of time you normally would spend writing feedback on students' papers.

and conferencing with them. Think of all the time you sit at home marking papers and giving them feedback. Fill as much meaningful, individualized feedback into a class as possible. This will eliminate hours of time you normally would spend writing feedback on students' papers.

It might seem like a lot of work, but I found that student-centred classrooms were far less exhausting to my pregnant introverted self than trying to capture and hold the attention of 28 teenagers for 48 minutes straight. I found it far more rewarding sitting one-on-one with a student and discussing how to fix her thesis statement than giving generic instruction to a group. And the best part is that students get the immediate feedback they need, and you are not lugging boxes of papers home every night to mark.

Students get the immediate feedback they need, and you are not lugging boxes of papers home every night to mark.

Fewer Tests, More Independent Work

One thing that I am trying to do as an experienced teacher is to give fewer tests. When I first started teaching 24 years ago, the Internet wasn't so prominent. I was all about having students regurgitate facts back to me. Now I really see that there has to be a shift on that. I can't just have my students memorizing things because, in the long term, they don't remember it. They remember it for a test and then they walk away and that is it. They were simply memorizing it to memorize it—to do well on a test but not to authentically understand it and learn content.

Now I have fewer tests and more independent work. Since I have been working for so long, I have my class routines and I can work with students while the rest of the class is working independently. I feel like with routines and expectations, kids can be more independent and that allows me to look and be observant of where they are. I can do one-on-one conferences with my kids and sit down and talk to them and listen to them. I feel like that is far more effective. I am trying to be more in the present. Since I am doing fewer tests it means I am not having to create my tests all the time, so that saves time.

I also used to do a lot of centres, which took a lot of time for me to prep. Even though I tried to give students direction, I still felt like I couldn't meet with kids because they are all so needy. Or I would get it going and then everyone would be in a centre and then I would not be able to pull anyone. Centres just didn't work. I was not able to reach as many students as I thought I was going to and I just thought there was too much preliminary work for me and then with all the worksheets from the centres, it was a lot of marking. This year I have started teaching *The Daily 5*, and I have a better system. Right now, we are in week ten of school and the only work that I take home are my anecdotals, or feedback to parents, or planning. –Jill, Grade 2 Teacher

Initially, I cautiously tried several tactics with my students. The following year, while on maternity leave, I read every blog and book I could get my hands on about teaching and learning. I connected professionally with educators through social media. I spoke about assessment at teachers' conventions and met teachers who shared their thoughts, struggles, and solutions with me. I looked at the long-range plans that I had been using for the past five years for Language Arts and tore them apart and put them back together again.

When I returned from maternity leave, I implemented these ideas about teaching and assessment full force. And consequently, I reduced the time I spent working outside of the classroom significantly. Once I accepted that it was within my power to have a better quality of life, the way I approached teaching began to rapidly change. I embraced the changes as proof that I was able to improve and refine my teaching skills at any point in my career and at any age. I hope you will embrace the changes too.

Now that you have a clear idea about key components of a thriving classroom, you are ready to explore life outside of your lessons, specifically how to maximize your prep time and your after-school time.

How to Give Helpful Feedback
(A Humorous Version for Students and Teachers)

Note: This is by no means a comprehensive list. You can generate a list of your own as well.

1. Avoid feedback that is too vague: "Needs Work!"

   (Well obviously it needs work, hence the entire editing process, thanks a lot.)

   Narrow it down further: "Avoid run-on sentences."

   No, even further: "You have 12 run-on sentences in your paper. Please find them and correct them." or "This is a run on sentence. Please break it down."

2. Avoid feedback that does not improve the quality of the paper: "Great vocabulary!"

   (While this is lovely to hear, it does not help make the writer better.)

   Instead try: "Great persuasive vocabulary in your opening, such as: 'catastrophic environmental consequences' and 'dire need.' Please include the same excellent persuasive vocabulary in your conclusion."

3. Avoid feedback that is too harsh (and/or personal): "This is the worst paper written in the history of humanity. And you wear ugly socks."

   No matter how catastrophic the writing is, please give the person steps to improve it: "This paper is lacking structure. Please go back to the outline and follow the recommendations given there."

So feedback should be specific. It should improve the quality of the assignment. It should not be too harsh or strongly worded.

Peer Editing: Persuasive Essay

Author: _____

Editor: _____

Introduction

1. State the hook:

2. Give the hook a mark out of 5 for its effectiveness: ____/5. Explain.

3. State the thesis:

4. Give the thesis a mark out of 5 for its clarity: ____/5. Explain:

5. List the two supporting points and the rebuttal in the introductory paragraph (if there are missing supporting points or a missing rebuttal, make a recommendation):

   • Supporting Point #1:

   • Supporting Point #2:

   • Rebuttal:

Pembroke Publishers ©2019 *Teaching Well* by Lisa Bush ISBN 978-1-55138-337-8

Peer Editing: Persuasive Essay

Body

1. State the topic sentence for the first paragraph of the body:

2. Does the topic sentence match supporting point #1 in the introduction?
   YES   NO

3. State the topic sentence for the second paragraph of the body:

4. Does the topic sentence match supporting point #2 in the introduction?
   YES   NO

5. List 5 detailed, relevant facts in the body of the essay (if there are not five, make recommendations):

   -

   -

   -

   -

   -

Pembroke Publishers ©2019 *Teaching Well* by Lisa Bush ISBN 978-1-55138-337-8

Peer Editing: Persuasive Essay

6. List 5 emotional words in the body of the essay (if there are not five, make recommendations):

   -

   -

   -

   -

   -

7. List any distracting facts, quotes, or sentences that need to be removed:

   -

   -

Rebuttal

1. Is the third body paragraph a rebuttal style argument?   YES   NO

2. Identify the following parts of the rebuttal:

   - the strongest point:

   - the weakest point:

   - an overlooked point:

Pembroke Publishers ©2019 *Teaching Well* by Lisa Bush ISBN 978-1-55138-337-8

Peer Editing: Persuasive Essay

Conclusion

1. Is there a conclusion?   YES   NO

2. List emotional words, if any, used in the conclusion:

   •

   •

3. List any new facts or irrelevant information that should be removed from the conclusion:

   •

   •

4. Give a mark out of 5 for the conclusion's effectiveness. Use the criteria below as a guide: _____/5

   • 1: Off topic/irrelevant/no conclusion.
   • 2: Restates the thesis or some of the key points.
   • 3: Restates the thesis, gives two reasons, and a rebuttal in a straightforward—but let's face it—somewhat boring way.
   • 4: Restates the thesis, gives two reasons, and a rebuttal in a straightforward, somewhat interesting way.
   • 5: Wow! I want to jump out of my chair and shout "Hurrah!" in agreement with this AMAZING conclusion. The writer has completely won me over to her/his side.

5. Are the sources listed at the end of the essay?   YES   NO

One final piece of advice to give the author:

_____

_____

Pembroke Publishers ©2019 *Teaching Well* by Lisa Bush ISBN 978-1-55138-337-8

Public Speaking Unit – Preparation

Name: _____

Since a key component to public speaking is being prepared, one-third of your overall mark is based on what you do before your formal class presentation. These feedback forms must be completed in detail and submitted at the time of the presentation.

Presentation/Visual Feedback #1

Three strong points of the presentation/visual	Three recommendations for improvement of the presentation/visual
1.	1.
2.	2.
3.	3.

Date of practice presentation: _____

Total time of the practice presentation: _____

Name of evaluator: _____

Pembroke Publishers ©2019 *Teaching Well* by Lisa Bush ISBN 978-1-55138-337-8

Public Speaking Unit – Preparation

Presentation/Visual Feedback #2

Three strong points of the presentation/visual	Three recommendations for improvement of the presentation/visual
1. 2. 3.	1. 2. 3.

Date of practice presentation: _____

Total time of the practice presentation: _____

Name of evaluator: _____

Pembroke Publishers ©2019 *Teaching Well* by Lisa Bush ISBN 978-1-55138-337-8

5

Preps and After-School Time

Optimizing Your Prep Time

On a scale of 1 to 10, with 1 being horrendous, and 10 being spectacular, the amount of time that teachers have during the school day to plan for their classes is negative 10,237,999. I sincerely think the person who determines how much time teachers have during the day to plan has

a) never taught a day in their life; or
b) not taught in the last two decades and has no long-term memory (and therefore has no recollection of all the time needed to plan).

If you teach in Canada, chances are that the amount of time that you have to plan was the result of pleading, threatening, begging, and toeing the line between your teachers' union and the provincial government. Ultimately, politicians are the ones who conceded to your planning time requests (so the answer is "a").

I will tell you who is *not* deciding what is adequate planning time for Grade 5 teachers: Grade 5 teachers. I will tell you who is *not* deciding what is adequate planning time for middle school Math teachers: middle school Math teachers.

For the majority of us, the amount of time we have to plan for our classes is ridiculously inadequate. As our student population becomes increasingly complex, the amount of prep time allocated to us *should* increase. Unfortunately, that is usually not the case. I am telling you this so that you know that the below recommendations are not *instead of* talking to your teachers' union and writing your politicians about the importance of teacher planning time. It is to do *in addition to* being vocal about the importance of teacher planning. And being vocal does help. In the mid-1970s, there were no preparation time clauses in any public elementary collective agreements in Canada. Preparation time was allocated arbitrarily. In 1987, 9,600 brave teachers in Toronto went on strike. They used the slogan "It's About Time." It was the Toronto strike that forced the provincial government to take the issue seriously.

Today, in Canada, many provinces have set preparation time for teachers. It ranges significantly from the relatively common 240 minutes per five-day week to the vague, "The Employer will make every reasonable effort to ensure teachers are provided preparation time." As of 2014, elementary teachers in British Columbia had a pitiful 90 minutes per week. Which is approximately *18 minutes a day* to e-mail, call, plan, prepare, assess, assist, organize, collaborate, create, update, discuss, and document. Seriously. In reality, 18 minutes is about the amount of time I need to pee (we often have line-ups in our staffroom bathrooms), wash my hands, refill my water bottle, and go back to the classroom.

Regardless of your prep time, it is essential to maximize your productivity during preps in order to reduce the amount of time you spend working after school hours. So here are a few tips that will save your precious (and most likely inadequate) prep time.

Create To-Do Lists

Many of us use our planner to chart our daily lessons in detail. However, if you are like me, you might be leaving your preps blank. Only in the past two years did I start to create detailed "to-do" lists for preps in my planner. It made a significant difference in my focus and efficiency. Before your day begins, plan out how you will use your preps. Make a list. Write it down.

Group Tasks

Some collective agreements stipulate the minimum amount of time allotted for a prep. For example, some agreements might stipulate that a prep has to be longer than 20 minutes, so if you have a 15-minute break while your students go on recess, it does not count as prep time. This is valuable, as 50 minutes of uninterrupted time is far more productive than three 16-minute preps. But in my experience, preps are not long enough. And because our preps are usually quite short, it is a good practice to group your activities together. For example, during one prep, answer all pending e-mails and clean out your e-mail inbox. During another prep, plan. This is more effective than trying to do three or four unrelated activities in one short period of time.

On a similar note, avoid single trips to the photocopier. Instead, photocopy everything you will need for the next few weeks during one trip. You will be surprised at how much time this technique saves. I found that by photocopying in bulk, I could spend weeks without even going into the copier room.

The same idea applies for trips to the office. One trip to the office—after running into a co-worker or discussing an impromptu issue with an administrator—can (and often has) taken 50 minutes. So group trips to the office. If you have to go, submit your field trip form, stock up on sticky notes, make a parent phone call, and sneak a fistful of chocolates from the front desk all in one trip.

Use Preps to Decompress

> We need time to gather our thoughts and compose ourselves in order to regain positive energy for the next group of students.

There are many, *many* preps that I have spent with the door closed, sitting down in a silent room staring at the wall, just trying to regroup after a particularly hectic day or a particularly challenging class. If you need a prep just to decompress, go for it. Drink water. Put your feet up. Close the classroom door. Put your cell phone away in a drawer. Listen to relaxing music. Or listen to nothing at all. Turn off the fluorescent lights. These are productive preps as well. We need time to gather our thoughts and compose ourselves in order to regain positive energy for the next group of students.

> It is a lot easier to be kind, compassionate, and loving when we are in touch with our soul.

By simply relaxing, staring at a wall, and listening to the ambient sounds from the building, you can clear your mind and rid yourself of some of the stresses of the day. Sometimes by just *being*, by sitting for a moment we can get in touch with our inner spirit, our soul, our inner being. It is a lot easier to be kind, compassionate, and loving when we are in touch with our soul.

When I asked Registered Nurse Lisa Hildebrand for the absolutely most effective thing that a teacher can do to calm herself after a hectic morning or a horrifically challenging class, she replied, "breathe." Simply taking five deep breaths in and out can make a huge impact on our stress levels. Most likely seeing my eyes rolling or my unimpressed expression, she went on to explain the *why* behind breathing:

Our autonomic nervous system is divided into two parts—the sympathetic and the parasympathetic systems. The sympathetic nervous system is responsible for our fight or flight response. Back in the days of cave people, this response was critical and life-saving. When faced with a stressful situation (like running from a saber-toothed tiger), the sympathetic nervous system kicked into gear and humans were able to run faster for longer and had a better chance of surviving an injury. Any type of stress will activate the system in the same manner. It could be the noise level in your classroom. It could be the fact that half of your class forgot to bring their books to class today. It could be the angry parent e-mail you received. When you feel stress, your sympathetic nervous system kicks into gear and a whole host of cascade effects happen, including the release of cortisol and adrenaline as well as immune suppression. Basically, your body perceives stress, and your body is in flight. Even though you know in your head, 'I have just had a rough morning with my students,' your body is running. So, all these systems go into gear to keep you running—to preserve your life. Like any temporary fix that is being employed as a long-term solution, the system starts to break. The organs and glands responsible for the sympathetic response begin to tire and eventually fail. Symptoms like difficulty getting up in the morning, inability to handle stress, afternoon energy slump, and poor immune function are just some of the many effects on the body.

The parasympathetic system is the flip side. It is responsible for digestion, healing, regeneration, and is the system that should be operating 98% of the time. Unfortunately, in our world right now we spend a whole lot of time in fight or flight mode, constantly bombarded by emotional, physical, and mental stress. Think of the last time that you were really relaxed. That is what it feels like to be in parasympathetic mode.

We spend most of our time in a sympathetic response, literally running for our lives. So, in that time of stress, you need to actively physiologically shift from one system to another. And you can do that just with breathing. And literally, five deep breaths where you are inhaling for five long seconds and exhaling for five long seconds will shift you from sympathetic response into parasympathetic responses that will calm you down. Your emission of cortisol will shut off. Your body will realize that you are not running for your life and all systems will slow down. So breathing is very powerful. You need to actively switch into that system, so you can sleep, digest, heal, and recuperate.

Since I had this conversation with Hildebrand, I have used spare moments during lunch or preps (or sometimes driving to school) just to focus on my breathing. I encourage you to do the same when feeling stressed.

Treat Paperwork like Paperwork

In her book *168 Hours: You Have More Time Than You Think*, Laura Vanderkam encourages readers to focus on their core competencies or the things that they do really, *really* well. These are things that are unique to us—things that other people cannot do skillfully or cannot do at all.

Core competencies could relate to career, home life, or wellness. For example, in my family, I am really, *really* good at fostering creativity in my children. We read books together. We sing together. We draw together. We fabricate stories together. These are all things I am good at and I enjoy doing. On the other hand,

I am not particularly fantastic with teaching my children specific athletic skills—nor do I enjoy it. So I outsource sports. My children take their gymnastics lessons, or rock-climbing lessons, or soccer lessons at our local community centre.

For the sake of this section, let's apply core competency to our work. Our core competencies are our areas of strength. In the right work environment, they bring us joy and fulfillment. They are the things we should devote most of our time and energy to while at work. Everything else in our job, according to Vanderkam, can be outsourced, ignored, or minimized.

When it comes to teaching, most highly skilled teachers love (and are really, *really* good at) creating learning opportunities for students. They love making connections with students. They love creating safe and supportive learning environments. I have yet to meet an excellent teacher whose core competency—the thing that sets her apart as a stellar educator—was paperwork. So, by all means, let's spend as little time as humanly possible on paperwork that does not directly impact student learning.

Be efficient with your paperwork. Whether it is individualized progress report comments or specialized programming plans, communicate what needs to be communicated, document what has to be documented, and move on. Minimize the time you spend on it. Devote as little time or energy to it as possible. Take one prep where you close the door, focus your energy on completing the task, and be done with it. Move on so you can have time and energy for what matters the most in teaching—your interactions with your students.

Report Card Comments

I was out of the classroom for eight years while running my own company. This year I returned to teaching on a full-time basis and I feel that my time away from the school setting gave me a fresh perspective of what teachers were doing. What I noticed is that the new teachers are just frying themselves. They look at report card comments and it would be a paragraph or two about every single child that they taught. Whereas for the more seasoned teachers it would be a sentence or two. Very direct comments—things that the kids can work on, things that they are doing well. And that was enough. I think that teachers need to see that enough is enough and you don't have to go to the ends of the earth for every single task.

Focus your energy on having a well-thought-out unit. One that gives students opportunities for creativity, self-exploration, and going beyond the objectives. This is the crucial part of teaching. The other stuff, you don't have to put a ton of time into it.

–Sara, Grade 1–12 Teacher

Be Intentional

When I returned to teaching full time, my daughter Catherine was 12 months old. I left the house in the morning before she was awake (my husband took her to daycare) and her bedtime was 6:30 pm. I knew that if I wanted to see my daughter, I needed to come up with a plan. So, I spent one to two nights working late at school—some nights I stayed as late as 8:00 pm. All other days I left the building the moment school was out. By 3:00 pm, I was driving out of the staff parking lot. This way I was guaranteed quality time with my daughter three nights a week, on the weekends, and during winter and spring break. No guilt attached. I rarely brought work home with me.

Regardless of your family situation, be intentional with your after-school time. If you have any preps or spare moments in the afternoon, spend a few minutes tidying up your classroom before the end of the day rolls around. If you have things that must be done before you leave, make a list and get to it. Then leave. Go home. Go for a walk. Avoid spending time in the hallways having non-essential conversations with co-workers. If necessary, once students are gone for the day, close your door to help focus yourself and discourage conversations.

Make an afternoon schedule that works for you. Are you running the yearbook club every Monday after school until 5:00 pm? Then promise yourself that on Tuesday and Wednesday you will leave school as early as possible to give yourself some free time to take care of yourself or do what you are passionate about. Whether it is getting a kick-ass workout at the gym, doing some writing at a local coffee shop, or spending time with your own children, make it a priority. If you see some co-workers on your way out smile, wave, and wish them a great afternoon. No one will see it as impolite if you don't stop to talk.

Set up a Marking Routine

Remember that guilt I discussed at the beginning of the book? The guilt we feel when we lug a pile of papers home five nights in a row and lug them right back to school the next day unmarked? Well, stop lugging papers home five nights a week!!! Find a marking routine (this includes a time and a place) that works well for you and stick to it. All other nights and weekends, the marking stays at school.

For example, I found that marking at home did not work for me. Instead, I preferred to spend one to two nights working late at school. This schedule worked really well not only for me but also for my students. Whenever they asked, "When will our short stories be marked?" instead of giving my previous response, "Heck if I know…" I could say with confidence, "Next Thursday night is my marking night. So you should have them by Friday."

Find a schedule that works best for you in regard to marking. The non-scheduled days, leave your marking and your guilt behind. Ensure that you are marking at a time when you can think clearly and there are no distractions.

Ask Yourself:
- What time of the day do I have the best focus for marking? Early morning? Afternoon? Evening?
- What environment would be ideal for marking? Is it free of distractions? Is it an enjoyable environment for me to be in?
- How many hours a week of undisturbed marking time do I really need?

Extracurricular Activities

Teachers are asked to do a heck of a lot outside of contracted school hours. These after-school activities have positive implications for our society and students. However, extracurricular activities can also be imposed upon teachers without consideration for the toll it takes on our lives or the lives of our families.

In 2012, Ontario proposed Bill 115, a law that would limit teachers' bargaining powers and right to strike and would impose a 1.5% pay cut in the form of three unpaid professional development days. Bill 115 was followed by years of austerity measures that prompted teachers to act in various forms of protest. In 2015, the Elementary Teachers' Federation of Ontario responded in a powerful way. As a form of protest, elementary school teachers put a temporary halt on extracurricular activities. This form of protest caused outrage by the general public. One Canadian journalist ranted that teachers were "sticking it to students," and "holding after-school activities hostage."

Teacher advocates such as Misha Abarbanel noted, "You wouldn't work extra hours for no pay, why should teachers?" Society is quick to notice what families are losing when teachers do not participate in extracurricular activities. Yet teachers have families too. When too much is demanded of them without being financially compensated, the desire to coach a basketball game at 8:00 pm also decreases.

Interestingly, the expectation that teachers should also be coaches is fairly unique to North America. When educational journalist Amanda Ripley studied countries that had widespread academic success, she noticed that in several high achieving countries sports were separate from school. In countries like Finland, Germany, and South Korea, parents or outside organizations ran sports teams at community centres—not at schools. When she asked one teacher in Finland if she knew any teachers who also coached, the teacher could only think of one explaining, "Teachers do a lot of work at school and that's enough, I guess." Ripley explains that when sports become entrenched in schools, principals have to hire teachers who can coach (or coaches who can teach), which can jeopardize the integrity of the teachers hired, and students are now expected to spend time before or after school training (as opposed to reading or studying). Ripley notes that, "Combined with less-rigorous material, higher rates of child poverty, and lower levels of teacher selectivity and training, the glorification of sports chipped away at the academic drive among U.S. kids."

Even though the presence of sports at school has not been proven to be beneficial to academic success, teachers are expected to pitch in and help. The Ontario teachers did eventually go back to after-school activities. In 2016, Bill 115 was deemed unconstitutional by the Ontario Superior Court of Justice. However, the message is clear: For now, in North America, teachers are expected to participate in extracurricular activities, despite our expanding responsibilities and growing complexities in our classroom.

There will be years when you have loads of energy and want to take on new projects—including after-school activities. Other times, minimizing school obligations is essential to your well-being. There is a season for everything. Allow yourself to scale back professional obligations when you feel you just can't hack it. One consultant at a recent meeting voiced her alarm at how tired and worn out teachers around our district looked. And it was only November. She reminded us, "You must put yourself first. Then your family. And then your students." We must remember this. And live this. Especially when it comes to hours beyond class time.

If you are stressed about cutting back on extracurricular activities, talk to your administration and explain your situation. Regardless of whether it is due to physical illness, mental health, family issues, an unusually challenging class or workload, or just plain old burnout, a good administrative team will be supportive. Highlight what you have contributed in the past, and what you hope to contribute in the future once you are physically and mentally able. Often, when we are proactive and confide in our administration, we are rewarded with compassion and support.

That being said, if you plan on teaching for a while, you will be expected to participate in extracurricular activities at some point in your career. Find what interests you and dive into it. If your school does not offer anything that ignites a fire in your soul, start your own club or group.

One teacher at our school was a marathon runner. She started a running club. She spent two afternoons a week doing what she loved the most—running. This was an activity she would have been doing regardless—the only difference was this time she had 15 teenagers running with her. Don't sign up for something because you feel like you have to. Do something with students that invigorates you.

In previous chapters, we explored how to create a culture of wellness within our school and in our classroom. We have explored how to maximize our time within the school day in order to have thriving classes. We have looked at how to minimize the work that we need to do outside of school hours. Next, we'll take a look at how we can cultivate a healthy life beyond school walls.

Shifting Expectations

Shift Our Expectations of Teachers

A few years ago, we had, friends of ours, Juan and Luz, over for dinner. Juan and Luz were both teachers from Andalucía, Spain and they were on a three-year exchange program in Alberta. Juan was teaching at a bilingual middle school near our house. It was several months into the school year, and Juan was already fed up with our North American view of teaching. As we sat around the glow of the fireplace having cocktails, Juan began his rant on his teaching experience in Canada.

"It is *expected* of you; I keep being told." He said to us, gesturing emphatically as his Rioja swirled dangerously close to the rim of his wine glass. "I ask, 'Do I have to do this?' and I am told it is *expected*. It is *expected* of you to coach wrestling. It is *expected* of you to tutor students after school. It is *expected* of you to organize trips and events."

You see in Spain it is *expected* of teachers to teach. Not organize middle school spring dances, not coach badminton, not take kids on overnight trips to the zoo to observe nocturnal gorilla behaviors. But teach. Juan ended his rant by saying, "I am so tired I feel like a wet tissue someone has crumpled up and thrown on the ground!"

I think at this point in his speech I stood up and applauded. Juan had a right to rant. According to a 2011/2012 national study, teachers in Alberta spend on average over 60.8 hours a week on work-related activities. This is ten hours more per week on average than teachers in other provinces! Teachers spend 13.9 of those hours on work that we bring home, which is equivalent to nearly two extra days of unpaid work per week if a 40-hour work week is the benchmark.

At some point, in North America, we have to shift the way we view educators. Teachers are no longer expected to be just teachers (which is not an easy gig to begin with). In addition to teachers, we are now sex education experts and anti-anxiety counsellors. We are the digital citizenship police, basketball coaches, and chaperones for overnight field trips. We are cultural ambassadors and school dance supervisors. We are translators and autism experts.

Teachers have a huge impact on students' lives. But a teacher also deserves to have a life of her own. And I think in some cultures, we lose sight of that fact. We need to realize that, yes, our job is important and has great value, but our personal life is important and should be valued as well. We need to shift the idea that a "good teacher" is someone who is at school at 7:00 am and still there at 7:00 pm. We have to shift the idea that the busier and the more stressed a teacher is, the more devoted she is to her career. We need to acknowledge that a teacher can have a life outside of the classroom and still be an excellent educator.

Not only do we have to shift the perception of teachers' roles in education, chances are that we also need to shift the way our family perceives us, our friends and loved ones perceive us, and very likely the way we view ourselves.

The Little People in Your Life

If you carefully reduce the time you spend marking significantly, only to spend that time driving your daughter to soccer practice five times a week, or only to allow your son to take up his eighth musical instrument, it is not contributing to *you* living a life outside the classroom.

All too often I see teachers spending countless afternoons and weekends chauffeuring their family around the province to games, matches, tournaments, and competitions. Just keep in mind that you have worked hard to create this extra time—you deserve this time. You need this time to take care of yourself and keep yourself well. It is essential that your family understands that your physical, mental, and emotional needs are just as valid as theirs.

If, after discussing extracurricular activities with your family, you decide that the 6:00 am ice times on the opposite end of the city are essential to your daughter's success, come up with a plan for how *all* members of the family are going to pitch in to support your daughter's hockey schedule as well as your own schedule of daily wellness. You could possibly take her one morning and your partner the other. Your daughter will need to pitch in and make everyone's lunch the night before and do the dinner dishes, for example. If your family is all on board, own your decision. That means no complaining about how you *have* to drive across the city at 6:00 am. You do not have to, you *decided* to. If your family is not willing to help, no deal. It is not your sole responsibility to carpool all members of the family to their various activities.

You must get your family on board with your wellness goals. It will make you a better spouse and a kinder and more compassionate parent. As psychologist Simone McCreary points out, a common challenge for people with demanding careers is managing their emotions in their home life. It is difficult handling stressful work situations for eight or nine hours straight and then coming home and navigating family relationships. By taking an hour out of our day before we go home to go for a jog, we are much more likely to be the kind of parent or spouse that we want to be. Emotional regulation is much more difficult at home when we carry all of the day's stresses home with us without dumping it off at the gym or taking the time to decompress at some point throughout the day before coming home.

Friends and Family Members

Make sure that others in your life honor and respect your time and your pursuit of wellness just as much as you do. No matter what your age or family situation is, your time is valuable. It deserves to be respected.

The same could be said for the friend of yours that likes to vent day after day. After day. After day. For hours at a time. She might not be wanting advice or help. She just wants to talk. And talk. And talk. About her problems. Or your parents down the road that expect you to drop everything to spend weekends with them as you "don't have anything better to do." I was single for the first 30 years of my life and found it frustrating that family members expected me to spend impromptu weekend events with them since I "did not have anything better to do" (i.e., have my own family and children). I still find it maddening when it is perfectly acceptable for my brother to go into his law firm to work on a weekend while family is visiting but the same acceptance is not given to me retreating to my study for a few hours to write when family is in town. Make sure that others in your life honor and respect your time and your pursuit of wellness just as much as you do. No matter what your age or family situation is, your time is valuable. It deserves to be respected.

Surround yourself with friends and family members that uplift you and encourage you to be a better version of yourself. I have a group of three girlfriends that were my first friends when I moved to Canada. We all live very busy and separate lives, but we make a point to get together every few months for dinner. When we finally say goodbye at the end of the night, my face is sore from smiling and laughing. We discuss travel, literature, spirituality, fitness, food, and meditation, among other things. They are three very fun-loving positive people who radiate optimism and empathy. Don't get me wrong, we have gone through family deaths together, serious illness, and intense work challenges. However, even in difficult times, we build each other up. These are the types of people that we need to keep very close to our hearts. These are also the kind of people that we need to aspire to be.

Be the Voice for Your Wellness

Making time in our personal and professional life can be one of the hardest things we do. What we have to do is to become a voice for our own wellness. And sometimes we have to be a loud and persistent voice.

Back at work full-time with a one-year-old and a three-year-old, time is my most precious commodity. Walking in my front door after a day of work looks something like this: I open the front door lugging my laptop bag, lunch bag, and purse. Before crossing the threshold, I cautiously peer into the house. I try to be very, *very* quiet. For one brief moment, there is relative silence. I brace myself. Half a second later, my one-year-old son James comes tearing around the corner. Upon seeing me his entire face lights up. At lightning speed, he crawls over and pulls himself up. He hugs my legs and buries his head in them, doing a reasonable impression of a burrowing mongoose. Seconds later he is no longer satisfied with simply burring himself in my pant legs. Now he is simultaneously pulling my pants and screaming for me to pick him up. While I am mentally trying to figure out what to do with my bags while my son holds my legs and screams, my daughter Catherine enters. She runs full force into me. Not completely accidentally, she slams her brother out of the way. He collides with the floor while she screams MOMMY! MOMMY! MOMMY! MOMMY! MOMMY! MOMMY! ... (you get the idea). She yanks my pants. My son pulls himself off the floor and rams into his sister using his head. Which is rather large. When she does not move from the grasp of my legs, James wedges himself between Catherine and my legs. The two of them cling to me.

Abandoning hope of making it to my entry closest to hang up my coat and store my work bag, I throw everything on the floor and act as a human jungle gym for the next half an hour until I can flag down my husband and kindly request him to deliver a cold beer to me on the kitchen floor.

So often our attention goes to who or what screams the loudest. My two kids have this figured out. They know that the one who screams and pulls and pushes and yells for my attention will most likely get it. This also applies to tasks. Run out of clean clothes to wear for work? The laundry is screaming to be washed. Have no food to eat in the house? Groceries are screaming to be bought. Progress reports due tomorrow morning? They are screaming to be written.

What are the things that you find deeply fulfilling and meaningful to your long-term well-being? These things won't scream for your attention. At least not right away. Miss a Pilates class at the gym today? Silence. Didn't spend time writing today? Or yesterday? Or the day before that? Silence.

Your children will not have a meltdown because you missed a gym class. Your principal will not call you into the office and give you a lecture because you did not spend 30 minutes last night on your creative writing. No one is screaming for you to get these tasks done. Yet these things may arguably be some of the most important things in your life.

What will happen is that little by little our physical and mental wellness will get buried. It will get buried under deadlines and required tasks. It will get buried under the things and people in your life that are screaming for your attention. And it might take months or even years before you start to feel a loss. It is as if a part of your soul has been extinguished. It is a silence and darkness that you feel.

We have to be the voice for our wellness. We have to "scream" for it. A three-year-old has no issue yelling the top of her lungs "MOMMY! MOMMY! MOMMY!" Likewise, we have to yell out into the world, "TIME FOR ME!" While the professional in me is clearly being metaphorical with the term "yell", the wife in me has used this tactic multiple times, much to the horror of my husband and children. And while I do not recommend it (it is not particularly conducive for relationship building), it does get the point across: My wellness matters.

Share the Workload

My favorite anecdote from my much-loved copy of *Lean In* is when Harvard Business School Professor Rosabeth Moss Kanter was asked at a conference what men could do to advance women's leadership. She replied, "The laundry." Professor Kanter's response makes sense when you think about the statistics: when a mother and father are both employed full time, the woman does 40% more childcare and 30% more housework than the man. This can be disastrous not only for a woman's career but also for her finding time to maintain her own health.

If you have a partner or spouse who lives with you, and you both are working about the same amount of time in your careers, you should also be spending relatively equal amounts of time on household and family obligations.

Your own personal wellness is going to be much more challenging if you are the one getting your children dressed, taking them to daycare in the morning, picking them up after work, driving them to swim lessons, preparing dinner, doing the dishes, making lunch for the next day, and putting them to bed without support from your significant other.

Ask Yourself:
- Do I have an equal partnership with my partner?
- What responsibilities need to be adjusted so all family members have equal time for wellness?
- What responsibilities can be minimized? (Do I really need to sweep the floors every night? Do I need to bathe my small children every day? Could I carpool with other families to school?)
- What responsibilities can be outsourced? (Could the family eat out once or twice a week to have a break from cooking and cleaning? Could I hire someone to come in once a month to clean?)

Note: For single parents, a huge *shout out* to you right now. I think you are awesome and amazing. Some of the single moms in my life who are very close friends are also some of the most healthy and well-rounded people I know. So, doing this solo and fostering your wellness is *possible*. It is difficult as all get out, but possible. However, if you are in a partnership with someone else, it should be just that: *a partnership*.

One thing that I found helpful in the early years of marriage was to make a list of all the things that needed to be done to run an organized household. Then Enrique and I sat down and each took turns initialing off on one task we would be responsible for. We went back and forth until the list was completed, divided evenly between him and me. See Regular Household Tasks on page 103 for a list you might want to share with your partner. Now ten years into marriage we do not use the list as our responsibilities are engrained in us. However, I refer back to this tactic when we have a new large time-consuming task ahead of us such as selling our house and moving or going on a lengthy trip. This way, no one person gets swamped with hours of work.

Focus on Priorities

Every Sunday morning during the winter months, I take my three-year-old daughter to our community aquatic centre. For $3 (and 25 cents for the lockers) we spend two hours in the steamy indoor pool. We leave the biting cold and the frozen ground behind us as we enter the hot, humid swimming area. And we float.

I have watched my three-year-old daughter transform from clinging with an iron grip to the side of the pool to independently pushing herself out the side and swimming lap after lap. Sometimes she will just lie in the pool and float. Other times she experiments with what her body will allow her to do in the water: she flutter kicks, scissor kicks, does backstroke, and sometimes she just practices rolling from her back to the stomach. She submerges herself under water until she hits the bottom and pushes herself up, gasping for air as she reaches the surface.

I currently live in Canada, 3,300 kilometres north of where I was born and raised. Growing up in Jackson, Mississippi, summers were synonymous with the smell of chlorine, sunscreen, and heat. During the winter months, I practiced daily with the city's competitive swim team. I can't remember a time when I was not swimming.

Ask Yourself:
- What is precious to me?
- What matters the most?

Focus on a handful of aspects: your health, your career path, quality time with family. Focus on these things and minimize other distractions in your life.

These two hours every Sunday are the highlight of my week. Not only am I spending time giving my undivided attention to my daughter, but I am preserving some of my own childhood tradition. Living in a country where I feel horribly inadequate in my ability to teach my children how to ice skate and ski, explain the rudimentary rules of hockey, define curling, or even build a snowman (I had to get our babysitter to teach my kids), I think: *Swimming—this is something I can do*.

Swimming is a tier one priority. Every Sunday my calendar is cleared for swimming with Catherine. And as soon as James is old enough, he will join our Sunday morning tradition.

The Importance of Reading

Reading is essential to me. I read every single night when I go to bed. It does not matter if I go to bed at 8:00 pm or 10:00 pm or 2:00 am, I always read for at least 20 minutes. Mostly with the book falling on my head by the end. It's two things, I think. One is to escape the day. To escape into this book and into this world. If it is a good book I can't wait. When I make my bed in the morning, I say, "I will see you later, I can't wait." And those characters stay with me all the time. When I finish a really good book I mourn that book for weeks. I think about the characters. I think about what they went through. I wonder how they are doing. I wonder if there is a sequel. So partly it is to cocoon away from the day and escape. And the other thing is pleasure. I read for the sheer pleasure. So, I read all the time. Now that my kids are older I have time to actually read on a weekend. I sit down with a cup of tea for an hour and just read.

–Lorelie, Grade 7, 8, and 9 Teacher

Don't Try to "Have It All"

Trying to "have it all" is about as productive as wishing for eternal youth. One thing that I have learned is that I can write a book OR I can have a decorated house with a beautiful garden. I, personally, have not figured out how to do both without driving myself and my family nuts. So I focus on what is important—my family, my health, and my writing. In the process, I try to let the fact that my front yard resembles a wilderness preserve or the TV room looks like a laundromat exploded not get to me. I give myself permission by saying loud and clear (in my head), *Lisa, this is not a priority.*

Stop Trying to Have It All

I did something—I dropped the class for my master's degree that I was taking. I wanted to do something for me because if I am going to be there for my kids at school, and my own kids, and my house, I have to be well. Both emotionally and physically.

So my master's is on hiatus right now. People tell you, "Oh you can do it all." And we can't. We absolutely can't. There is a lot of pressure and most of the pressure we put on ourselves.

I find that I am so foggy because I am trying to do so much. I am missing appointments. I just can't keep it all together. And I am not myself. And so, I quit. I quit my class. And I am so overjoyed with my decision. Who cares? I can pick it up later. I am happier. I went to yoga last week. Since I stopped this class, I feel this weight lifted on me. And I was putting all that pressure on myself.

–Dawn, Grade 7, 8, and 9 Teacher

Recently we had a massive series of errands to run and minimal time to do it in. Mostly because I hate errands. I wait as long as I can and only tackle them when I can put them off no longer. Even then I often try to get them over with as quickly as humanly possible in one large marathon attempt. We went to Goodwill, two friends' houses to drop off used baby items, the library, the gas station, car wash, the bank, and the grocery store in under two hours.

During this time, I was fully aware that I would see friends and most likely see students or parents of students while out and about. And yet during this marathon errand mission, in my frantic attempt to get out of the house and get these errands over with before lunch and the children's naptime, I was wearing sweatpants with some undetermined yellowish brown stain on the front (we will say it was mustard), fleece socks from my university days with impressively large holes in the bottom, and gardening boots caked in dirt. My hair was unbrushed and I was wearing no makeup. At one point I mentioned to my husband that I looked like an extra from *The Walking Dead*. He heartily agreed. When I started to panic at the state of my appearance I just said to myself, *Lisa, today this is not a priority*.

Next time you start to panic at the state of your desk, or the state of your bathroom floor, or the fact that you have not managed to do (insert any random task here that is stressing you out), just say to yourself, *This is not a priority*. By saying that you are acknowledging that your desk or your bathroom floor is not in as great of a condition as you would like it to be. However, you are intentionally letting it go. By not spending time on the small things and by not stressing over the small things, you are preserving your time and energy for whatever it is that matters to you. Having said that, once you have taken care of your wellness needs, take care of the things that have to be done.

On a similar note, get comfortable with mediocrity in some areas of your life. Specifically, in the areas that are low priorities. Make beautiful sculptures, but mediocre green bean casseroles. Get comfortable with imperfection.

When I asked Registered Nurse Lisa Hildebrand how she managed to work as a nurse, raise three children, and run her own medical practice, her response was that we have to let things go. She focuses on the essential elements that need to get done and lets the rest go. Hildebrand says:

> For me, it is really about letting the insignificant things go. If the sink has dishes in it, and it is 11:00 pm, I leave those dishes and go to bed. Or if the laundry is piling up and everyone is out of underwear, I say, 'Okay now I am going to do a load of whites to get everyone's underwear, but I am not going to conquer all of that today because other things need to happen.'
>
> I think that women have this need to do it all perfectly and nobody else is feeling that pressure. Our husbands are certainly not feeling that pressure, we don't want our children to feel that pressure, so we need to take the pressure off ourselves. Stop *should*-ing yourself. *I should be…I should be…I should be…*there is never an end to what needs to happen in your day. Not when you are working full time and running a household and raising kids. There is always something you could do. Instead, do something for yourself. Do something that fills your bucket. Sure you would love to clean out the storage room in the basement, the bookshelf is overflowing, the fridge needs to be wiped down. All of those things will still be there. The dishes will wait. The storage unit will wait.
>
> In my weeks, I get the things that I need to get done, done. I make lists for the week. These are the five things that HAVE to get done for the week. And that is my focus for the week. And I work on them throughout the week. And at the end of the week when I actually do those five things I feel quite good. I feel like I have accomplished something. It reframes your focus to what you did do as opposed to all the things that you did not do.

Categorize Your Priorities

Ask Yourself:
- What would I classify as "tier 1 priorities?" (These are things that you find deeply fulfilling and meaningful to your long-term well-being. Things like family, health, a creative endeavor.)
- What would I classify as "tier 2 priorities?" (These are things that you enjoy but are secondary to tier 1. Like having a well-maintained home or an active social life.)
- Finally, what would I classify as "time wasters?" (Netflix, social media, and negative gossip with co-workers are some examples. Try to eliminate these as much as possible from your life.)

When making daily to-do lists, keep track of how many things are necessary but have little long-term impact on your life (e.g., vacuuming, laundry, grading papers) versus items that will have a long-term effect on your mental and physical health (e.g., 30 minutes of writing, going to the gym). Make time *each day* for one or two of your long-term goals that promote wellness. Put them at the top of your to-do list as opposed to the bottom as the last priority after everything else is done. After all, what are the odds you will be in your 80s thinking to yourself, "I had such a fulfilling and rich life. All that lovely time spent dusting…"? Priorities.

Psychologist Simone McCreary asks, "What is the core of what needs to happen and then what can actually happen? Many of us have 300 hours' worth of demands that we put on ourselves in a 168-hour week. Something has to go."

Exercise as a Priority

Exercising is something that I will do every day no matter what. If I have to get up at 5:00 am to do it, I absolutely will. And if that means I have to go to bed at 8:00 pm in order to fit it in, then that's what I will do. With teaching your brain does not turn off during the school year. It's always going. In order for me to relax and take a mental break, I exercise. It's my time to mentally check out.
–Vanessa, Grade 5 Teacher

Sleep as a Priority

One thing that I was not prepared for with teaching was how time-consuming it was outside of your structured paid time. And that it still a constant balance to find. Over the years you find tricks and things that work for you in order to keep the balance. I know there are certain things that I need to do on a Sunday to set myself up for the week or else I just feel chaotic all week. Like I have to go to bed just a little bit earlier so I feel rested because I know my days can be long and exhausting.

I am not willing to compromise my sleep. If I am not rested, it does not matter how great my day was planned or what fabulous lesson I had going. If I don't have the energy to execute it, it all falls apart. Sleep is something that I need to keep the balance.
–Tara, Grade 5 and 6 Teacher

Down time as a Priority

I have to sleep. I cannot *not* sleep. So sleep is definitely a priority. I also need down time—even though I live alone. Being with kids all day long sends my noise-level tolerance into overdrive. I need quiet time. I can't keep going. I need "me, myself, and I" time at the end of each day. If I have to work at school, I will lock the door and have my back toward my window.

Sometimes down time is a 20-minute power nap—that's good. Since I'm in graduate school I just don't have the energy to read a book. And now that I have to wear glasses, anything that I can do that does not involve my glasses is good too. I just need quiet time. If it is not too hot, I will just sit on the balcony and look out at the rainforest.
–Jill, Grade 2 Teacher

Keep Self-Care Times as Sacred

Since self-care is a key component to our mental and physical health, we must start viewing these times as sacred. I have found it helpful to set specific times and get it on paper. Physically putting it down can be helpful. Otherwise, it can easily get placed on the back burner. I cannot do it today, but I will tomorrow. Or next week. Or after winter break. Having a plan as to how to make time for yourself and troubleshooting when obstacles arise (which they will) is very helpful. For example, if your self-care plan involves going for a 30-minute walk after school, what happens to your wellness time if you have an after-school meeting or event? Can you make some time for yourself at the end of the day to take that walk? Or can your partner get the kids up and dressed that morning and let you go for an early morning walk? Setting specific times and making plans for troubleshooting when obstacles arise will make your wellness goals more attainable. Especially for people who are really busy. Prioritize what is important to you and make sure it has a spot in your daily schedule.

After speaking with McCreary this summer, I actually decided to "practice" my morning gym routine before returning to school in the fall. And it is a good thing I did! The first two days when my alarm went off at 5:15 am I immediately turned it off and went back to sleep. The third day I made it to the gym, but after an hour of running, drenched in sweat, I realized that I left my toiletries at home. So off to the store I went to buy a second round of shampoo, conditioner, and soap to leave permanently in my gym bag to avoid that mistake again. I knew that if I did not troubleshoot my early morning gym routine before school started, I was much more likely to get flustered and abandon my routine once I had a non-negotiable deadline of being at school at 8:00 am than if I had it already practiced and implemented it. Now a month into the new school year, my gym routine is an ingrained part of my day. I love it!

If a few years ago a full-time teacher with a busy life outside of school said to me, "I take time every day for myself," I most likely would have thought *that's impossible!* But in reality, it is not as difficult as we think. If daily self-care of some sort seems impossible or too time-consuming, put it into perspective. One activity that McCreary recommends to those that like to see things visually is to lay out your week in 60-minute or 30-minute segments so you can get a good picture of how much time you are working and how much time you are sleeping. Color coding it will help you to visualize how much time you spend on each task. And give yourself permission for taking care of yourself—there should be enough time for purple (or whatever your self-care color is). Check out pages 104–105 for a Sample Self-Care Chart that you can use to track your time.

Shift Our Expectations of Ourselves

In order for society to change its perception about teachers, we have to change the way we view ourselves. Do you expect to be the perfect teacher, the perfect best friend, the perfect girlfriend or boyfriend, spouse, parent, employee, and/or co-worker? Do you expect that everyone will be happy with your decisions and your work at all times? In my experience, this type of thinking is one of the quickest paths to a nervous breakdown. It also leads to a very restrictive lifestyle that is not one bit conducive to creativity or empowerment.

In order for society to change its perception about teachers, we have to change the way we view ourselves.

Get comfortable with choosing a path of teaching and a path of living that are not the status quo.

Get comfortable with choosing a path of teaching and a path of living that are not the status quo. The more I have consciously made decisions to find my own path in life, the more I have been comfortable with disapproval and even with confrontation. For someone like me, who has always viewed myself as a "pleaser," "non-confrontational," "quiet," and "introverted," shifting my self-perception was huge. I mean really huge. In the ninth grade, I gathered up the courage to play on the girls' soccer team. During one game I had a clear shot at a goal. I sprinted to the ball and inches away from it I came to a halt just in time to let a member of the opposing team steal the ball. After the game, my mom asked me why I stopped right in front of the ball, and I replied, "I did not want to hurt the girl's feelings. So I let her have the ball." Needless to say, I put my energy toward non-competitive activities after that.

Simply making decisions and following through such as, *I will leave school today at 3:00 pm* or *I will not volunteer for 45,000 after-school activities this year*, terrified me. Requesting from my family that I have time to write a book constantly ruffled feathers, believe me. But ultimately, I had to shift my expectations for myself and the way I viewed myself. I stopped seeing myself as someone whose job was to please others. Instead, I became someone who wanted to be my full self. I became a person that *is* honest and aware of the equal humanity in other people. But not obligated to please them.

Regular Household Tasks

Initials	Task
	Buying groceries
	Preparing breakfast
	Dishes (breakfast)
	Preparing lunches
	Cooking dinner
	Dishes (dinner)
	Unloading the dishwasher
	Wiping down countertops/stovetops/appliances
	Sweeping floors
	Vacuuming
	Dusting
	Emptying garbage/recycling/compost
	Cleaning out the refrigerator/freezer/pantry
	Cleaning bathrooms
	Mopping floors
	Tidying up the house: toss clothes in hampers, have kids put their toys away
	Sorting/putting away mail/important paperwork
	Sorting/washing laundry
	Folding/putting away laundry
	Ironing
	Mowing the lawn
	Watering the yard
	Weeding/planting the garden
	Getting car serviced
	Handling day-to-day finances/investments
	Waking the kids up
	Getting kids dressed/ready for school
	Taking kids to school
	Picking kids up from school
	Organizing kids' playdates/sports/activities
	Taking kids to playdates/sports/activities
	Helping kids with homework (older children)
	Bathing kids (younger children)
	Getting kids ready for bed: pajamas/brush teeth (younger children)
	Putting kids to bed
	Getting up in the middle of the night with children (younger children)
	Taking time off of work to be with sick children

Pembroke Publishers ©2019 *Teaching Well* by Lisa Bush ISBN 978-1-55138-337-8

Sample Self-Care Chart

☐ Sleep ☐ Family time ☐ Household chores ☐ Errands ☐ Work ☐ Meals/meal preparation ☐ Wellness

	Monday	Tuesday	Wednesday	Thursday	Friday	Saturday	Sunday
5:00 am–6:00 am							
6:00 am–7:00 am							
7:00 am–8:00 am							
8:00 am–9:00 am							
9:00 am–10:00 am							
10:00 am–11:00 am							
11:00 am–12:00 pm							
12:00 pm–1:00 pm							
1:00 pm–2:00 pm							
2:00 pm–3:00 pm							
3:00 pm–4:00 pm							
4:00 pm–5:00 pm							

Pembroke Publishers ©2019 *Teaching Well* by Lisa Bush ISBN 978-1-55138-337-8

Sample Self-Care Chart

☐ Sleep ☐ Family time ☐ Household chores ☐ Errands ☐ Work ☐ Meals/meal preparation ☐ Wellness

	Monday	Tuesday	Wednesday	Thursday	Friday	Saturday	Sunday
5:00 pm–6:00 pm							
6:00 pm–7:00 pm							
7:00 pm–8:00 pm							
8:00 pm–9:00 pm							
9:00 pm–10:00 pm							
10:00 pm–11:00 pm							
11:00 pm–12:00 am							
12:00 am–1:00 am							
1:00 am–2:00 am							
2:00 am–3:00 am							
3:00 am–4:00 am							
4:00 am–5:00 am							

Conclusion

One Tuesday night this past January, I was sitting in bed with Catherine reading her a bedtime story when I glanced up to see my husband stumble by—he had just put James to bed. As he passed the doorway I noticed he was clutching his chest. I heard him mutter, "I can't breathe" as he moved out of sight. I shot out of bed and trailed behind him down the stairs where he collapsed onto the couch. I immediately called 911. Enrique was having a heart attack.

My daughter stood beside me watching in silence as our small entryway filled with paramedics. Enrique waved to Catherine while being wheeled down our driveway strapped in a gurney and loaded into an ambulance. The next few weeks were a blur. The temperature was hovering at about −30°C and skies were a continuous grey. While there were periods of time during those weeks that I do not remember, I do remember the constant feeling of cold as I scrambled to arrange full-time daycare for my two small children, organize family compassionate leave with my school, and drive across the city to visit Enrique in the hospital. However, one morning while driving on the highway toward the hospital, I remember with surprising calm and clarity thinking to myself, *Well. I guess I really have to focus on wellness now.*

For us, a young immigrant family living in a country where our nearest relative is one border crossing and over 3,000 kilometres away, wellness is not a luxury, it is mandatory. Our one-year-old son and three-year-old daughter are depending on their parents to be healthy and alive for decades to come. I share this with you to illustrate how overnight my ideas of wellness shifted from an important, but nevertheless abstract ideology, to a very physical, tangible pillar of my life. Every personal and professional decision from whether I should apply for an administrative position to what we should have for dinner tonight is made with wellness at the core of my consciousness.

Two days after Enrique's heart attack I showed up at our neighborhood daycare centre to beg the director to take our two children full-time starting immediately. They had room for my youngest, but no available spot for Catherine. I was wavering between relentlessly begging and simply slumping down onto the floor and not moving until they agreed to take my daughter. As appealing as lying on the floor sounded in my exhausted state, I decided to go with relentless begging: "Please take her—she is a wonderful child! And very quiet. And small! You will hardly even notice she is here!" Very probably, in order to get me to shut up, the director said, "Okay. She starts tomorrow." And turned to her desk to gather the necessary paperwork. Then unexpectedly she turned back to me and said, "Lisa, you have to stay strong." And then again, "Stay strong."

And that is the best piece of advice I have been given in a long time.

As educators who affect the lives of children in a very real and direct way, we have to stay strong. We have to stay healthy. We have to stay positive and compassionate. After the heart attack, determined to regain my own strength, I was willing to go down paths I have never travelled before—regular therapy visits, meditation classes, and opening up to my friends and co-workers in a very vulnerable way. And now my job as a teacher is more important than ever. Because I want Enrique to be able to work part-time or even retire when his health demands it, I value my job more than ever. And since I will probably be working at it longer than I expected, I better be enjoying it more than ever!

Just as I have become a stronger individual, my focus at work is fine-tuned into what truly is important, which has made me a stronger teacher. I have honed in on the anxiety, insecurity, joy, or gratitude of my students and co-workers. I try to focus on "how I can make [insert person's name]'s day better? What does [this person] need today?" as opposed to "What do I need to get done today? What do I need to cover today?" And I am even more ruthless with finding ways to cut the administrative tasks that cut into our days and offer little or no benefit for ourselves and our students.

I hope this book has given you the courage and the knowledge of how to make wellness a pillar in your life, in your classroom, in your school, and in your family. I hope it has given you the courage to hold wellness close to your heart and say with conviction and empowerment, "I deserve to take the time to stay strong and healthy. I am worth it." Because you are. I wish you a successful path on your wellness journey. And please, stay strong. Stay strong.

Acknowledgements

I could not have written *Teaching Well* without the help of colleagues, friends, and family. I would like to thank Mary Macchiusi for seeing the potential in my manuscript and having the vision to take it on as a project. I cannot thank you enough for your guidance with this project. I would also like to thank Alisa Yampolsky for being the kind, insightful editor that we all dream of working with. And many thanks to all those at Pembroke Publishers—you are a fantastic team!

Many exceptional educators contributed to this book. They took time out of their weekends and afternoons to sit with me and talk about their personal and professional experiences. I thank the extraordinary teachers whose interviews are a part of this book: Vanessa Briere, Kate Cordell, Mark Driedger, Tara Ehret, Sara Haney, Lorelie Haydt, Kath Moors, Jill Rivers, and Dawn Vaessen. A big thanks to Rebecca Brewer, Megan Cowan, and Melissa Thompson for sharing your lesson ideas with me.

I would like to thank Lisa Hildebrand and Simone McCreary for helping me on my personal physical and psychological path to wellness. And a special thanks to Christine Brownell who is not only a close family friend but an amazing mental health nurse and educator. The three of you are caring, compassionate individuals whose insights helped shape this book.

Special thanks to my family: four generations of educators have instilled in me a love and passion for education. Thanks to my aunt and inspiration Sharon Haffey, who told me that I needed to write this book. And thanks to my mom Joan Jones, for her reading and early feedback on the manuscript. Finally, thanks to Enrique, Catherine, and James. You are my reasons for embracing wellness.

Professional Resources

The following are all books that I read while doing research for this book. They range in topics. But they all played an influential role in inspiring me to reduce my own workload, improve my teaching, and focus on my life outside of teaching. I would like to share them with you.

Alberta Teacher Workload Study. https://education.alberta.ca/media/3114984/teacher-workload-study-final-report-december-2015-2.pdf

Brown, Peter C., Roediger, Henry L., & McDaniel, Mark A. (2014) *Make it Stick: The Science of Successful Learning*. Cambridge, MA: Harvard University Press.

Burgess, Dave (2012) *Teach Like a Pirate: Increase Student Engagement, Boost Your Creativity, and Transform Your Life as an Educator*. San Diego, CA: Dave Burgess Consulting, Inc.

Csikszentmihalyi, Mihaly (1996) *Creativity: Flow and the Psychology of Discovery and Invention*. New York, NY: Harper Collins.

Doyle, Terry & Zakrajsek, Todd (2013) *The New Science of Learning: How to Learn in Harmony with Your Brain*. Sterling, VA: Stylus Publishing.

Dweck, Carol (2006) *Mindset: The New Psychology of Success*. New York, NY: Ballentine Books.

Froese-Germain, Bernie. "Work-Life Balance and the Canadian Teaching Profession." Canadian Teachers' Federation. https://www.ctf-fce.ca/Research-Library/Work-LifeBalanceandtheCanadianTeachingProfession.pdf

Fryer, Bronwyn (2006) "Sleep Deficit: The Performance Killer." Harvard Business Review, October; 84(10): 53–59.

Gallo, Carmine (2014) *Talk Like TED: The 9 Public-Speaking Secrets of the World's Top Minds*. New York, NY: St. Martin's Press.

Gilbert, Elizabeth (2015) *Big Magic: Creative Living Beyond Fear*. New York, NY: Riverhead Books.

Irvine, David (2016) *Caring Is Everything: Getting to the Heart of Humanity, Leadership, and Life.* Calgary, AB: Gondolier.

Kestin, Janet & Vonk, Nancy (2014) *Darling, You Can't Do Both: And Other Noise to Ignore on Your Way Up.* New York, NY: Harper Collins.

Kirr, Joy (2017) *Shift This!: How to Implement Gradual Changes for MASSIVE Impact in Your Classroom.* San Diego, CA: Dave Burgess Consulting, Inc.

Lucas, Lisa J. (2018) *Practicing Presence: Simple Self-Care Strategies for Teachers.* Portland, ME: Stenhouse Publishers.

Lyman, Linda L. (ed) (2016) *Brain Science for Principals: What School Leaders Need to Know.* Lanham, MD: Rowman & Littlefield Publishers.

Miller, Donalyn (2009) *The Book Whisperer: Awakening the Inner Reader in Every Child.* San Francisco, CA: Jossey-Bass.

Ngozi Adichie, Chimamanda (2017) *Dear Ijeawele, or A Feminist Manifesto in Fifteen Suggestions.* New York, NY: Alfred A. Knopf.

Rainbow Kennedy, Susan Ariel (2004) *Make Your Creative Dreams Real: A Plan for Procrastinators, Perfectionists, Busy People, and People Who Would Rather Sleep All Day.* New York, NY: Simon & Shuster.

Ripley, Amanda (2014) *The Smartest Kids in the World: And How They Got That Way.* New York, NY: Simon & Schuster.

Ripp, Pernille (2016) *Passionate Learners: How to Engage and Empower Your Students.* New York, NY: Routledge.

Sackstein, Starr (2015) *Hacking Assessment: 10 Ways to Go Gradeless in a Traditional Grades School.* Cleveland, OH: Times 10 Publication.

Sandberg, Sheryl (2013) *Lean In: Women, Work, and the Will to Lead.* New York, NY: Alfred A. Knopf.

Stroud, Gabbie (2016) *Fixing the System.* Griffith Review (51) https://griffithreview.com/articles/teaching-australia/

Taylor, Dr. L. (2018, January 30). Personal communication.

Torrance, E. Paul (ed) (1963) *Education and the Creative Potential.* Minneapolis, MN: University of Minnesota Press.

Vanderkam, Laura (2010) *168 Hours: You Have More Time Than You Think.* New York, NY: Penguin Group.

Index